THE
NEW
CELIBACY

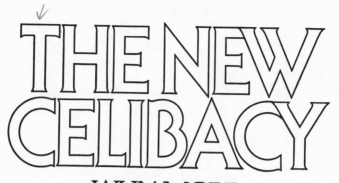

THE NEW CELIBACY

WHY MORE MEN AND WOMEN ARE ABSTAINING FROM SEX— AND ENJOYING IT

Gabrielle Brown, Ph.D.

McGraw-Hill Book Company

New York   St. Louis   San Francisco
Toronto   Sydney   London
Mexico   Düsseldorf

1 2 3 4 5 6 7 8 9 BP BP 8 7 6 5 4 3 2 1 0

LIBRARY OF CONGRESS CATALOGING IN PUBLICATION DATA

Brown, Gabrielle.
   The new celibacy.
   Bibliography: p.
   1. Celibacy. I. Title.
HQ800.B64   306.7   79-28847
ISBN 0-07-008430-0

Book design by ROBERTA REZK

For my parents

He that on earth from birth to death observes chastity,
for him there is nothing beyond reach,
know this, O herdsman of men . . .

from the VEDAS

Contents

THE
NEW
CELIBACY

As the Pendulum Swings: Some New Signs of the Times

1 CELIBACY. Most people are actually celibate most of the time, yet when they hear the word "celibacy" they think only of priests, nuns, and certain repressed bachelors from bygone eras. But celibacy today is emerging as a much broader concept. So even those of you who are already slightly alarmed by the title of this book can rest assured that, with a little further understanding, it is possible to see celibacy as the basis for sex, not its opponent. If one is good, the other is not necessarily evil.

The first question is: What would anyone be doing as a celibate *now*—at the grand finale of the sexual revolution? That would be like going on a diet just when the banquet was finally served. Nevertheless, for many people, sex after the sexual revolution is just about as exciting as football the week after the Super Bowl. Too much of a good thing reduces its charm.

A group of people who were currently celibate discussed their nonsexual preference on a nationally televised *David Susskind Show* in October 1978. Some saw their choice as the result of a lifestyle that required a constant juggling among activities where time was precious. Most, however, saw it as a reaction to the "overkill" of the sexual revolution—in order to escape what was seen as the high pressure, the merchandising, the waste of time and energy. They wanted to avoid what they called The Sex Biz—to get away from it entirely. They did not want sex to be the basis for relating, with its emotional malnutrition reflected in an all-too-common experience of going to bed with people who were strangers. They concluded that sex is vastly over-rated; that throughout the nation people are no longer re-pressed and, therefore, that the "media hype" of sexiness and sexual attack is no longer valid; that a sense of a more spiritual rising consciousness is the emerging trend, and that the pendulum is now swinging the other way.

In his history of sexuality in America, Milton Rugoff points out that today "sexual liberty has not automatically brought sexual fulfillment." Once you've enjoyed sexual freedom and done everything you've ever wanted to do (and even some things you didn't want to do) and asked every question you ever wanted answered, read the books and mastered the positions, you may still feel unfulfilled. Two hours later, you're hungry again and the sexual revolu-tion doesn't seem to be over but you are: not exactly spent but definitely ready for something more. Or something less. Once everything has been tried, even if you are giving all your waking and dreaming energy to new sexual activities, there really is no *original* sin left. Except perhaps the social sin of not sinning at all. Sexuality has become, according to Rugoff, disassociated from "all those qualities that have made it most precious: the intimacy, sympathy, and warmth of a one-to-one relationship, the sense of cherishing someone and being cherished above all other individuals, the sense of maximum commitment."[1]

Like so many things in American culture, affluence of sex has depreciated the value of sexuality and undermined the very essence of good sexual encounters. Results of this devaluation of sexual love are turning up in some surprising places:

• The sex magazine *Penthouse Forum* (January 1979) reported that sex is now too easy to have and therefore has become an often meaningless experience.

• *The New York Times* (May 1, 1978) reported that a wave of "asexuality" is sweeping the nation as an antidote to traumatic sexual experiences such as divorce and the pain of casual sex.

• On a New York City television news report, a group of devoted disco dancers revealed that they enjoy the dancing more than sex and say that when they go home to bed these days, they go to sleep.

• *The Village Voice* (January 23, 1979) reported that the latest vogue is to "come out" as celibate. Noted among the celibate "chic" are Mick Jagger (who says that it avoids a lot of problems) and Andy Warhol (who finds cracking jokes in bed more fun than having sex).

In the entertainment field, the overwhelmingly sexual orientation of the past two decades may also be subsiding. In movies sex tends to have become more subdued, replaced by other more awesome inventions. *Jaws, Close Encounters of the Third Kind, Star Wars,* and *Superman* have been among the biggest recent hits and the least sexually focused. Even in the more sexual movies, such as *An Unmarried Woman* and *Coming Home,* sex is no longer exploitive—rather, it is sweet, loving, funny, genuine.

At the discos, an evening of uninhibited dancing is said to hold greater fascination than an evening of uninhibited sex. And in 1978 a trend was reported among young Punk Rock followers: The kids were "bored by sex." They could have it just about as much as they wanted, but they weren't interested. At age fifteen, it was old hat. As one musician told *The Village Voice*: "Discos are killing sex and Punk Rock is driving the final nail into the coffin."

Dancers, artists, and actors are the primary groups reported to be turning from sex, but even politicians are being singled out as emerging "nonsexuals." San Francisco columnist Charles McCabe described Governor Jerry Brown as "conspicuously celibate," while *The Village Voice* supposed that New York's Ed Koch is "the first asexual mayor."

This growing interest in celibacy follows an earlier renewal of respect for virginity. Whereas during the 1960s virginity was considered an embarrassment at best, during the 1970s it staged a minor revival. More young girls were reported to be less willing to be pressured into the complications of a sexual affair for which they were emotionally unprepared. Due partly to the impact of the women's movement, they were more likely to resist pressure from their peers.

There were even women who wanted to revert to their prior "virgin" status. In his research on "secondary virginity," Dr. Joel Moscowitz of Columbia University found that "After a period of promiscuity that they find disillusioning, they became scrupulously chaste, saving further sex for marriage or at least for an emotionally close and stable relationship."

In 1972, an organization called The American Virgin Liberation Front was written up in an article in *Esquire*. Taking off on the other liberation movements, its goals included establishing freedom for those who wish to refrain from sexual activity; removing the stigma attached to chastity; and instilling in virgins a sense of pride.

In the mental health field, the lack of sexual interest (called "inhibited sexual desire") is now considered the number-one patient complaint. In one study of married couples reported in the *New England Journal of Medicine* in 1978, one-third of the couples said they had sex two or three times a month or less; in another study, reported in the *American Journal of Psychiatry*, one-third of the married men and women were sexually abstinent on the average for two months at a time and many for three months and longer.

Noting a growing national trend among both single and married people toward less sex, members of the American Association of Sex Educators, Counselors and Therapists reported that as many as half their patients considered the lack of sexual desire their primary reason for seeking counseling. This was contrasted with previous primary concerns of patients, which had been premature ejaculation, impotence, and inability to have an orgasm—known as "performance criteria." Now, according to these therapists, the *desire* to perform is also problematic, especially among young adults in their twenties and thirties. The patients are said to have good sexual response when they do have sex, but they may desire to have it only once every six months. They seek therapy because they feel something is wrong with them and/or that their lack of desire is causing stress in their marriages. Some therapists conclude that there is something to be concerned about. Noted sex researcher Dr. William Masters and Dr. Helen Singer Kaplan, director of the human sexuality program at New York Hospital–Cornell Medical Center, both see this phenomenon as the result of a generally more open acknowledgment of all sexual concerns. They and some other sex therapists tend to view this reduced sex interest as pathological. They see it stemming from hostility, depression, anxiety, and other sex-inhibiting neurotic restrictions. Kaplan states: "For some people, sex is fraught with so much anxiety, anger and negative emotion that it may be a better adaptation not to risk it."[2] And, according to Dr. Otto Kernberg, director of a psychiatric hospital in Westchester County, N.Y., what a couple may describe as boredom with sex is really a cover-up for underlying rage and hatred in the marriage.

But other professionals take a different position. Sex therapist Dr. Shirley Zussman calls the new celibacy "a kind of support for saying 'no'." Researcher-author Shere Hite and psychologist-author Bernard Zilbergeld both noted that neither men nor women either need or want sex all that much. Under the social pressure to be more sexual, many may have denied their real desires to move toward less sexual activity, but now they regard their emerging celibate status in a very positive way. One actress found that her sexual appetite just fell away, not unlike her other "addictions" such as smoking and drugs. Others see celibacy as "a comforting antidote to . . . traumatic divorce, random sex and the pressure to 'score.'"[3]

Well, okay. Perhaps there is some lack of interest in sex these days. This doesn't mean that everyone is just turning off and becoming celibate. And what does it mean to be celibate anyway?

Before examining the various dimensions of celibacy, it will be helpful to look at sex today—what it is, why we are so heavily intrigued by it, and what we expect from it—to see why it is more often disappointing than fulfilling.

SEX TODAY

From the way we eat to what we drive to what we take in from the media, sex is an inescapable point of reference. Often, though one may not even notice it, there is a tendency to be dominated by sexual thinking to the exclusion of other modes of experiencing. Historians report that this massive sexual liberation is the natural release of a culture which has been horrendously repressed in its sexual life. America has moved from being the most sexually misinformed nation to perhaps the best (technically) informed. Americans easily participate in what not so long ago they considered the most unnatural of acts—and which is now often considered correct dating procedure. Eminently practical, we Americans took to "getting good" at sex with the same intensity with which we once denounced it.

Because sex has become *the* methodology for "Total Expression of True Love," love is now filtered through a great array of sexual techniques and expectations. As a result, sex today is no longer sacred.

Of course, this has been of great benefit to those for whom sexuality was unclear, mysterious, unrewarding, or frightening. In this regard, A. C. Kinsey, William Masters and Virginia Johnson, Shere Hite, and other sex researchers have our gratitude for providing valid, straightforward information regarding sexuality, enabling many people to enjoy sex perhaps for the first time in their lives. This new knowledge has provided other ways to think about sexuality. So it has actually been less a revolution in sexual activities than in "thinking about" those activities. Free of guilt, free of embarrassment, why shouldn't we enjoy sex?

Well, we do enjoy sex. But maybe we don't enjoy it as much as we are expected to nowadays. The overemphasis on sex takes our attention continuously to the sexual, bombarding each of us with all kinds of reasons to be taking advantage of the "new" sexuality. This leads to what sex researchers John Gagnon and William Simon call in their book *Sexual Conduct*, "an overenriched conception of sexual behavior." *People end up thinking they are more sexual than they really are.* And they feel they should live up to a false picture of sexuality that has been created as a standard. As Dr. Rollo May wrote (in his well-known *Love and Will*): "Where the Victorians didn't want anyone to know that he or she had sexual feelings, we are ashamed if we do not. . . . The Victorian nice man or woman was guilty if he or she did experience sex. Now we feel guilty if we don't."

The role of sex has also become further distorted by its overemphasis in the field of psychotherapy. A large number of therapists tend to encourage patients to dwell on sex at the expense of other, perhaps more pressing problems. And, in many ways, the psychotherapeutic field has ceased to function as a field but is now a specialization in sexuality. In California, for example, it has recently been ruled illegal for any mental health professional to conduct his or her practice without taking one particular state-sponsored course—a course in sexuality. (No other postcertification course is required).

One result of this narrowing vision is that the majority of people seeking professional help now conclude that their current state of unhappiness is caused by one sexual hang-up or another. Since sex is often used to relieve frustration that has occurred in another domain, it is not surprising that many men and women come to view all kinds of frustration as sexual. What may have been a very appropriate area of focus for the patients of Sigmund Freud in the mid-Victorian era has become today an overly significant focus for an already oversexualized clientele. As a result, there are many people who seek a sexual cause for every personal problem. They conceptualize their unhappiness in sexual terms.

Such people feel that if they could only solve their sexual problems, their lives would become more meaningful and fulfilling. This sexual approach to health and happiness within the therapeutic tradition is very misleading and restricts the potential treatment help. Dr. Harry Stack Sullivan admonished his colleagues, "Let me warn my fellow psychiatrists: If you want to do psychiatry that can well be crowded into a lifetime, see if you can't find something besides the sexual problem in the strangers that come to you for help. . . ." And Carl Jung discovered that when patients brought sexual questions to him, they invariably turned out to be religious questions.

To combat this overemphasis on sex, philosopher Elisabeth Haich suggests that the study of psychiatry include a personal experience of celibacy. "If a certain period of abstinence was prescribed, purely as an experiment, at universities, Western psychiatry would be plagued by fewer misconceptions!"

Besides its mental health value, we are also led to believe that sex is "good" for us in the same way that healthy foods, exercise, meditation, and other things have been found to raise the quality and longevity of life. But this, too, is misleading. Biologically, we don't lose the ability to be sexual by not being sexual. And unless one is in a very weakened physical condition, one has the potential to be sexual all one's life. Yet the deceptive impression has been created that one must be sexually active to remain healthy. The "use-it-or-lose-it" school of sexologists exploits fears of growing old to the fullest by making it seem as if sexual performance were the true test of youth and aliveness. (Actually, many cultures, particularly Eastern cultures—as will be discussed later—believe that sex can have a *weakening* effect on the physical and mental abilities of people of all ages.)

In some instances, sex has become an item of barter for achieving levels of success in other nonsexual fields. Like money, sex is often used to buy and sell power, position and fame. In a number of business dealings, sex has been found to be a useful tool—the "consummation" of the deal. It is against this inappropriate use of sex that certain groups such as the women's movement have taken action.

The physical activity of sex has become America's dominant social activity. And even if you are not participating in every sexual opportunity that comes your way, you are at least supposed to be fascinated by its availability. Even if you don't "do it," you are supposed to want to. It's really a social challenge to make sure to keep up with the freedom being granted to all of us. Perhaps for this reason, a "swinger" quoted by Masters and Johnson in *The Pleasure Bond* says: "It *is* important to have done it, if only to discover it's unimportant."

With all this undue emphasis on sex everywhere, we may wonder how interested in it we really are.

How Sexual Are We?

It has been found that people don't need or even want sex as much as they think they do. According to the research findings of Gagnon and Simon, "It is demonstrable that sexual activity is in fact not a very powerful drive and the word 'drive' itself may be a misnomer."

We may be far less sexual than the proponents of sex-as-life would have us believe. Despite the freedom to pursue sexual activity that is now available, men and women haven't been found by researchers to have become *more* sexual. What has obviously changed are the social/sexual expectations. But, report Gagnon and Simon, the actual intensity of sexual activity has not increased.

In general, sexual response has been understood to be both biologically determined and socially learned. The biological view—best represented in the work of Freud and Kinsey—contrasts with the environmental view. According to sexual-learning exponents Gagnon and Simon, the sociocultural determinants of sexuality replace the biological. They have concluded that it is the nonsexual developments of childhood which lead to sexual development—that sexual activity is not biological or instinctual but socialized. They maintain that sexuality is actually that particular aspect of human development where the triumph of the "sociocultural over the biological level is most complete." And, in fact, there are "numerous social situations in which the reduction and even elimination of sexual activity is managed by greatly disparate populations of biologically normal males and females."

Philosopher Bertrand Russell concurred with this view fifty years earlier when he wrote:

> The word "instinct," in fact, is hardly the proper one to apply to anything so far from rigid as human behavior in sexual matters. The only act in this whole realm which can be called instinctive in the strict psychological sense is the act of sucking in infancy. I do not know how it may be with savages, but civilized people have to learn to perform the sexual act. . . . What is instinctive . . . is the impulse to learn it, and often the activity which would give satisfaction is by no means definitely predetermined.[4]

One is ruled neither by the body nor the mind but by a mutual interaction between the two based on evolutionary processes. It is clear that there is indeed a biological basis for changing sexuality. But although biological considerations are not negated, one could speculate that the biological response of human sexuality is not as fixed or rigid as other biological responses and, in its flexibility, it is able to be more easily influenced by sociological factors. In this regard, as scientist Carl Sagan has noted, the effects of the environment on learning may be extended to affect the physiology. As the intellectual experience changes, so does the physiology—and vice versa.

So, as our ideas and attitudes toward sex evolve, so do our physiological responses. What one's body desires in the way of a fulfilling experience may become more subtle, more delicate, less specific, less a question of need.

As a possible consequence, sex has been demonstrated to be less interesting to people who are more fully developed in all other areas. In his well-known studies of self-actualized people—people living more of their full potential than the average—Dr. Abraham Maslow found that sex was not a preoccupation within the self-actualized groups:

> Self-actualizing men and women tend on the whole not to seek sex for its own sake. . . .
> In self-actualizing people, the orgasm is simultaneously more important and less important than in average people. It is often a profound and mystical experience, and yet the absence of sexuality is more easily tolerated by these people.
> . . .
> Loving at a higher need level makes the lower needs and their frustrations and satisfactions less important, less central, more easily neglected. . . .
> These people do not *need* sensuality; they simply enjoy it when it occurs. . . .
> Once these lower needs are satisfied, they recede from consciousness, and there is little preoccupation with them.[5]

Dr. Maslow also reported that a self-actualizing person could be sexually abstinent with no harmful effects because he or she would be comfortable with the experience and not feel it as a deprivation.

So if it turns out that most people are not all that interested in sex, especially mature, self-developed individuals, what is the meaning of the sexual revolution and how do we experience the sexual "freedom"—the "unpinning"—that has now become the right of every "normal" American man and woman?

Mental Sex

It is truly mind-boggling to consider what a distance Americans have come sexually from a century ago. What is now sexually permissible may have been subject to the death penalty back then. Yet the ideal freedom of sexual expression that has been achieved is still insignificant. This is because sexuality is visually understood in terms of the physical acts of sex. "Perversion" in sex is likewise defined by the *behavior* displayed by the "pervert." But, in fact, physical sexual activity is the same everywhere with little real variation. After all, what can be put where and for how long is pretty much determined by nature in advance. So in talking about sexual freedom, one is really talking about mental and social attitudes toward sexuality rather than the physical activities themselves.

There is a very good reason for this. Sex is mostly mental anyway:

> What really matters are all the ideas and perceptions that make sex work effectively for us as individuals.
> —MASTERS AND JOHNSON

> It is not the body that causes sexual desire . . . but the intellect.
> —ELISABETH HAICH

> To unveil the flow of thought can . . . be an even greater sexual intimacy than physical nakedness.
> —ALAN WATTS

A kiss may indeed be still a kiss, but it's usually a promise of more to come. Without the mental script that accompanies it, a kiss is not necessarily enjoyable. If you don't agree, try being kissed at a party blindfolded, without knowing who's doing the kissing. The desire to know the giver of the kiss is far more intense than the experience of the kiss itself.

All sexual activity follows a mental score, a fantasy of Events to Take Place. And for an event to be sexual, human beings require far more than the physical acts. (Just ask anyone who has ever been raped.) It is the mental appreciation and its emotional orchestration that makes an event sexual. Breast and genital examinations and mouth-to-mouth resuscitation generally take place without sexual arousal, but in the right frame of mind, these acts become highly sexual. The mind makes a continuum, a "story," out of a succession of physical moments. So even given a series of potentially sexual physical activities without the necessary mental outlook, "the probability of something sexual happening will remain," note Gagnon and Simon, "exceedingly small."

In fact, sex in some instances is *entirely* mental. Most people have experienced intense sexuality on the level of fantasy without any external stimulation. The body is truly a secondary consideration. A fascinating example was reported by medical researcher Theodore Cole in the June 1976 issue of *Medical Aspects of Human Sexuality*. He found that a number of paraplegic men and women report orgasms reminiscent of those experienced before they became paraplegic—including the entire sexual-response cycle described by Masters and Johnson: excitement, plateau phase, orgasm, and resolution. Dr. Cole goes on to wonder how this occurs if all the afferent impulses to the brain have been interrupted by the spinal-cord injury. He concludes that the orgasm is "psychological" and emphasizes that all "orgasm depends heavily, if not entirely, upon psychological set, whether one is able-bodied or spinal cord-injured."

The fact that sex is predominantly a mental experience through which the body is manipulated means that it is pointless to argue that, as a sexual being, one is at the mercy of one's physiological responses entirely. "The urge to merge" sexually is a thought before it is an action. So in general people decide when it is appropriate to be sexual. In this regard, sex is not only a mental activity, it is also a *voluntary* activity.

As Masters and Johnson have observed, "In one respect sex is like no other physical process. It is the only physical process that can be denied indefinitely, even for a lifetime."

Sometimes we forget that being sexual is a choice. If we are feeling sexy, we think we have to "do something" about it; otherwise, we'll be repressing an uncontrollable physical urge that will lead to frustration and anxiety. Actually, there is no real need to be sexual so far as human physiology is concerned. If one is, fine; if one is not, fine. The desire will most likely subside. Unlike hunger, thirst, and the craving for intimacy—which are the real needs—physical sexual gratification is far less necessary than imagined.

For an adolescent, especially in our overstimulating society, sex may feel very "involuntary." It is new, it is exciting, it is completely overshadowing. Only gradually does one learn that one has mastery over sexuality just as one learns mastery over many experiences in life. We learn to control sexual behavior and not to be controlled by sexual feelings. We learn that we can choose to be sexual or choose not to be. In *Existential Sexuality: Choosing to Love* Dr. Peter Koestenbaum goes so far as to say: "Human beings are not by nature sexual . . . but choose to be so. Sex is a natural urge, but the role it plays in your life and the importance you attribute to it . . . is a matter of free choice."

Yet we are all heavily influenced in this choice. And the reason most of us decide in favor of being sexual as much as possible is because we've been taught that sex is the road to personal fulfillment. This is one of the most destructive myths about sex—that there is such a thing as permanent fulfillment on the sexual level.

No matter how great an orgasm one has or how great an orgasm one's partner has, sex does not bring fulfillment. And if something more permanent is desired in the expression of love and one does not even experience it, one may feel unfulfilled, even saddened by the sexual act. There is a clear psychological description of this feeling called "postcoital tristesse" or "sadness after sex." This may happen because, as Elisabeth Haich observed:

> Sexuality mimics love. It compels tenderness and embraces, it forces the lovers to hug one another, to allay one another's pain through the revelations of sexuality, as when true love is exchanged. What follows such experiences? Disappointments, a bitter after-taste, mutual accusations or bleak loneliness, feelings of exploitation and defilement. *Neither of the two gave true love but only expected to receive it, therefore, neither received it!*[6]

Many people believe that sex is the only way to become fulfilled and spend years searching for lasting happiness in sexual encounters. There is nothing sadder than the loneliness of the sexual seeker who continues to search for personal liberation in a series of static encounters. In this fixed pattern of behavior, there is always a feeling of futility, of going nowhere.

But the positive side of the seeking is the recognition that one is looking for something more. Obviously, the more you expect out of life, the more you expect out of sex. In the search for fulfillment, for a permanent state of happiness and joy, you may try everything. With each experience, you may be able to see some progress, at least on the level of understanding. It is this understanding that gives the feeling of growth and progress.

The Need for More

The desire for growth and progress is really a basic part of living—no matter what· you enjoy, you inevitably want more. You either have to get better at it, grow in it, or get more of it. A new dress or sport coat only satisfies for a short time until something else new to wear is desired. Even fame and success have to be continually renewed to maintain happiness. In the glory of tomorrow's dinner, tonight's dinner is forgotten. The satisfaction of mastering a Beethoven sonata may evaporate in the upcoming desire to learn a new one.

Similarly, progress is necessary in physical activity. Mastery of the body is an essential part of human achievement. Just look at how the records set during the Olympic Games continue to be broken every four years. No doubt training and attitude programs advance as well, breaking mental boundaries prior to the moment of breaking the physical boundaries. But the body has its limits, and goals are always established within those limits. So physical progress, although necessary and enjoyable, is finite. In fact, many human endeavors are finite. And it is important to evaluate our desire to progress in light of what is possible.

With some things—the ineffables, the open-ended infinites such as love, knowledge, creativity—there's no need to worry. There's plenty of room to grow and progress. But with some things that may seem unlimited but really aren't, one could get stuck trying to break limits in a world of limits until all that is left are pieces of experiences—incomplete and less and less satisfying.

The acts of sex are some of those things. You can only get so good at each act—there are only so many good positions; orgasms can only be multiplied to a certain limit. If we think of sex as a progressive physical activity, as a kind of Olympics in the bedroom where records must be broken and performance judged, sex is really limited to physical performance criteria. Yet even if we don't just limit sex in this way, like other finite experiences, sex requires progressive achievement to continue to be enjoyable. We have to feel we are having better and better sexual experiences, whether with one person or with a series of people. Without this progress, sex seems to lose its value.

Sexually, one can "progress" either with a particular partner toward richer and fuller sexual experiences or with a series of partners toward an increasingly more complex set of sexual experiences heightened by the variety itself.

If one's sexual attention is exclusively on one partner, there may be a kind of subtle progression through a series of detailed learning experiences until one "gets good at" every interesting sexual activity. As one becomes more and more knowledgeable, new experiences are called for—not only to satisfy recurring sexual desires but also to keep progressing in the creation of the sexual relationship.

A person may read all the books on sexuality to learn new positions and techniques of lovemaking; he or she may travel to exotic places to create new environments for the activities. One may create an environment of exotic erotica right in one's own bedroom with myriad design features installed to reveal new angles of sexual interest. Or one may venture into the College of Multiple Orgasm and achieve numerical Advances in Contraction, and Degrees in Intensity. But sooner or later, no matter how much you love your partner, you are going to get bored once you run out of ways to progress in sexual expression. This may not happen in a week of lovemaking, but it can easily occur after five or ten years of marriage. At that point, a couple may start to question the validity of their relationship—and whether they are really in love.

This is an all-too-common occurrence in marriage. And of course a great and tragic misunderstanding. For if the partners see sexual interest as the key to the entire relationship or even as a reflection of the quality of the relationship, they may convince themselves that the relationship is over, done for. In fact, they may have grown *beyond* the need for sex and the sexual level of relating for a time and it may indicate, as we shall see later, the right moment to start to experience each other on an entirely new plane of union in relationship.

But because the current pressure on a couple is to be sexual, they may feel compelled to "open" their marriage to others and look for sexual fulfillment with different partners in order to "save" the marriage.

Couples seeking further sexual progress as described above or single people looking for the "right one" or individuals seeking fulfillment through constant variety may choose to have sexual experiences with a number of different people. But here, too, progress and learning seem to continue only just so far. Then a person may well become bored with, say, one partner at a time or one partner for more than one night. Thus he or she may branch out to groups of people, new combinations of positions, and so on. To keep growing and having newer and newer experiences may start to replace the quality of the experience as the determinant of progress.

Another way to look at this pursuit of fulfillment through sex is to examine what can be called the Thrill Effect—a search for overwhelming excitement in sexual encounters.

Seeking "the Thrill"

"Uninhibited civilized people . . . may fall deeply in love and be for some years entirely absorbed in one person, but sooner or later sexual familiarity dulls the edge of passion, and then they begin to look elsewhere for a revival of the old thrill." Bertrand Russell's observation is corroborated by modern research. In her studies on romantic love, Dr. Elaine Walster found that "six to thirty months is the average duration of the kind of heart-stopping, I'm-about-to-faint romantic frenzy we all think of as being 'in love.' " Of the ten thousand people Walster questioned, most reported that the intensity of passion starts to diminish after a couple of years at most.[7]

According to several authorities, what many of us yearn for sexually is to recreate or at least re-experience the thrill and ardor of adolescent sexual love. With hearts pounding and pulses racing, adolescents approach sexuality as if approaching a mysterious deity. But, as psychologist Hugo Beigel points out, these "adolescent feelings . . . though recognized as precious, are rarely experienced in adulthood with the same ardor."

Another interpretation of this search for the thrill is that one mistakes the thrill of fear and anxiety that may have accompanied sex during adolescence for The Thrill itself. According to H. J. Campbell in *The Pleasure Areas: A New Theory of Behavior,* "the initial exquisite pleasure is predominantly autonomic rather than sexual." Thus, when people seek to recapture the excitement of adolescent sex in adulthood, it is not surprising that they fail, particularly if they are halfway over the fear of sex. If one is still fearful, interestingly enough, sex is still thrilling. This may account for the pursuit of new and unusual sexual activities replacing more ordinary pursuits as one grows more complacent about sex.

Some homosexuals have recognized that the more dangerous and hidden nature of homosexuality adds a dimension of thrill not found in most heterosexual encounters. And danger apparently helps heterosexual romance as well. Walster's study revealed that obstacles to love provide an important spur to passion and romance. The extramarital affair, parental disapproval, and other difficult situations were cited as aspects of love relations structured within external limits that excite longer-term romance. When it is forbidden, it's still thrilling. But as fewer and fewer acts are forbidden or considered dangerous in our sexually open society, eventually "the thrill" is gone.

"Transcendent" Sex

Substituting the sexual for the spiritual or vice versa in the attempt to become fulfilled is another common mistake. Much of Jung's psychoanalytic work explored the deep interconnectedness often experienced between sexuality and spirituality. If one happens to have a spiritual experience during sex, it is easy to confuse the two and conclude that the spiritual can only be recaptured through the sexual. In *Free and Female*, Barbara Seaman describes "transcendent" sex:

> Once an individual has experienced transcendent sex even once, it seems to change her (or him) for a lifetime, making her (or him) more spontaneous, more open, more confident,

more loving, more purposeful, more peaceful. Naturally enough, the desire to repeat such an experience becomes very strong. Many "promiscuous" persons are idealists in drag . . . who are searching—futilely, as a rule—for a replay of some transcendent sexual experience they once enjoyed.[8]

Let's say you have an experience of a transcendental nature that opens you fully and you feel as if you are taken to the far reaches of the universe or you have a strong feeling of timelessness and unboundedness. And let's say that you have this experience during a sexual encounter. Then you may conclude that sex is the sole avenue to the experience of going beyond your everyday boundaries.

In fact, this experience can occur and does occur in many life situations. Artists, scientists, writers—anybody who creates, people who meditate, religious people, young children, and many others have all reported experiences of transcending that often take place in very ordinary circumstances. In her book *Ecstasy*, Marghanita Laski documents a variety of such experiences, as does Maslow in his work on "peak experiences."

These moments of transcendence may indeed occur during sex or they may not. But we do ourselves and our lovers a great disservice if we continue to seek the spiritual experience of unboundedness only in the sexual realm. Because we've been taught to look for the earth to move during orgasm, we focus all our spiritual hopes on this one limited channel of experience. And in so doing we may eliminate more fruitful paths to obtaining the fulfillment we desire.

But once a person becomes aware that what he or she is seeking *through* sex is something *other* than sex, he or she may decide to take attention off sex entirely, in order to explore whatever else is available. This shift in attention occurs naturally as one gains increased satisfaction in other experiences—in the ability to love, in the development of creative expression, in the achievement of success in any activity. As one grows, one inevitably looks to experience the kind of profundity of expression enjoyed in all other parts of life. If the quality of sex doesn't measure up, sex begins to move out of the limelight.

This is a primary reason people entertain celibacy as a possibility at some time in their lives—because they want to experience and express something closer and more representative of their own nature than even sex. It can be thought of as the desire for something more eternal, more permanent. And when individuals start to desire this fuller kind of self-expression, everything they do has to be re-evaluated in light of these new desires.

FROM SEX TO CELIBACY

Celibacy is a state of life known only to humans. The fact that one *can* be celibate if one so chooses is an indication of the growth of freedom. Natural life has evolved from the state of determined sexuality experienced by the lower animals to a state of potential sexuality wherein human beings are free to choose to be sexual or not.

This book is principally addressed to those for whom celibacy may be chosen as a positive life experience, although not necessarily for a lifetime. But it is useful to distinguish among the various reasons for celibate living by describing each briefly.

There are really several kinds of celibacy, each of which has certain physical, mental, and social characteristics. What kind of celibacy is involved is determined by why one has become celibate. In addition, two main categories of celibacy can and ought to be distinguished. One is celibacy freely chosen and the other is celibacy based on repression and fear of sex. The latter may have been the reason for the sexual revolution; the former may be one result of it.

Life Celibates

Generally, when thinking about celibacy, most people think of the life celibate. Such individuals often seem very far removed from ordinary life. As such, "the figure of the celibate monk, the wandering ascetic, the hermit who has renounced the flesh has always impressed, astonished, fascinated, shocked, even outraged the worldly man."[9]

Yet most of our traditional knowledge about celibacy comes from that group of spiritual men and women who have made a total commitment to a celibate life for the sake of a higher goal, often religious in nature.

In certain religions and on some spiritual paths, a person may choose to be celibate for life in order to keep his or her attention on the most elevated levels of knowledge and experience in devotion to God. The purity and dignity of such a deep personal commitment to God found in the various traditions of religious celibacy often serve to inspire the society. In defining celibacy, the *Encyclopaedia Britannica* describes how the uplift of the society is brought about through the example of a spiritual life advanced by the function of celibacy: "The celibate is seen by the community as it would like to be seen by the gods."

The mystique of the life celibates is no doubt enhanced by their seeming indifference to sex in light of what they must be experiencing without sex. Often they appear to have transcended sex entirely. Even Freud, who could never seem to leave a sexually repressed rock unturned, admitted that many life celibates may have grown beyond ordinary sexual needs and desires. He wrote: "What they bring about in themselves in this way is a state of evenly suspended, steadfast, affectionate feeling, which has little external resemblance any more to the stormy agitations of genital love." However, as will be discussed later, not all celibacy in the name of religion produces such spiritually beneficial results.

Other than the religious life celibate, there are also life celibates who have found the rewards of their celibacy applicable to other higher life goals. The naturalist Jonathan Chapman, better known as Johnny Appleseed, is one famous example of a spontaneous life celibate whose life activity was inspired in its dedication to bettering humanity and the environment and, thus, he "sowed his seed" in a more universal way.

Life celibates are usually individuals who are physically, mentally, and socially self-sufficient and who have no real need of other people even though they may be devoted to helping others. But there is another dimension of celibate living—what could be called perhaps "secular celibacy"— that includes some aspects of religious celibate life and some aspects of everyday social life.

Secular Celibates

> Why do certain types of sexual behavior— particularly celibacy and virginity—seem to recur again and again at "higher" stages immediately after a generation of supposedly liberated men have come to renounce them?
>
> —HERBERT RICHARDSON

Apart from the solitary life commitment of certain religious and/or spiritually inclined individuals, celibacy has also been the basis for a number of "ideal" societies throughout history, including much of Eastern culture and certain key societies in Western culture—from Platonic idealism through the courtly or romantic love tradition of the Middle Ages through some nineteenth-century American utopian communities to modern times. This history will be explored in the next chapter. Yet even at present our own society is looking once again toward celibacy—at least on a temporary basis.

It is important to understand that times of celibacy can be beneficial to most people—even married couples—but that the benefits are most fully experienced when one has become celibate by free choice. By contrast, there are many of us who are physically celibate but not necessarily by choice!

Celibacy by Default (Or Why The Earth Isn't Moving for Me in San Andreas)

One obvious reason for involuntary celibacy is a lack of suitable partners. There are times in everyone's life when there is simply no attractive potential mate around. A widow, a widower, or divorcee may go for long periods adjusting to celibacy before finding another partner. Sometimes celibacy occurs even though sexual experience is intensely longed for, as in the case of a young student looking for a first partner or a "war widow" awaiting the return of her spouse. This can be called "celibacy by default"—one is celibate, but not by choice.

Another experience of physical celibacy is also by default—the result of neurotic personality patterns that forbid an individual comfortable participation in any sexual experience. In such people the fear of failure, rejection, "sinning," "getting dirty," whatever—is too great to allow sexual feelings to be expressed physically. Usually these individuals are immersed in a consuming mental sexual life, and even though they are physically celibate it is certainly not because they want to be.

Celibacy by Choice

If one is not free to choose to be sexual, neither is one free to choose to be celibate. Like sex, celibacy is really only valuable when it is freely chosen.

Celibacy and sex are interdependent. To be totally celibate is to be totally sexual, even if unexpressed. One is at home with both experiences but not overshadowed by either. If a man and a woman cannot choose freely to be celibate because sex dominates their lives so entirely, then they are not really choosing sexuality freely either. Each act of sex must be a real choice from the status of the fullness of celibacy. If one chooses to express this fullness in sexual activity, fine—but the choice is one's own. If one chooses not to express it in favor of maintaining celibacy, this too is a free choice.

The most important reason for becoming celibate by choice is that we recognize that we want to be. Just as one can decide to be sexual, one can decide to be celibate—for a day, for a week or two, for a month, even for a year.

And how do you know if it might be a good time for you to try a little celibacy? Well, one way to know is when it drops off—the desire, that is. . . . If your attention is not on sex, it's easy to be celibate. If, on the other hand, you are always thinking about sex and full of sexual fantasies, it might not be the right time to be celibate. In fact, if your attention is always on sex and you are not having sexual experiences, it might be most appropriate to become more sexually active. If you are not ready to be celibate, you could get hung up *trying* to be comfortable in that state and more and more sexual fantasies would be the result.

The best way to tell if you might be ready to be celibate for some time is if it feels natural.

Celibacy When the Time Is Right

Celibacy is not an intellectual idea. It is not an ideal. It is a state of life that may occur in some people in a natural way. If it is more comfortable not to be sexual than to be sexual, then it is a natural kind of celibacy. On the mental level, if one's attention is not on sex, that too is indicative of a natural time of celibacy. Sexual fantasies tend to drop off as one becomes more celibate, as one's attention moves to other sources of enjoyment in life. If, however, one is physically celibate yet always thinking about sex and full of sexual fantasies, celibacy may not feel natural.

A precondition for being celibate is probably a certain development in the physiology of the individual. There have been no studies as such on the physiological changes from sexual activity to celibacy, but celibate people report that it becomes increasingly easier to be celibate the longer one remains celibate. On the other hand, there is no evidence to suggest that the *ability* to have sex is ever lost through celibacy. (In fact, short periods of celibacy may be the best cure for sexual problems such as impotence.) What may be lost is the *desire* for sex. As one becomes celibate, one may first lose not one's sexual desires but the *desire for sexual desire.* In this culture, the possibility of losing the desire to have sex may be thought of as akin to quiet death. But nature is much better-natured than that; if the desire to have sex goes, celibate people say, it is because the desire for other, even more important experiences has replaced it.

For some people, becoming celibate means being in control of their lives. A realization may have come that sex is not as enjoyable as they would like, yet they drifted along in sexual activity anyway. But a time may come when the desire to be true to their own desires enables them to take hold of their own lives and decide to say no to sex for a while. Some of us arrive at islands of sexual activity on a lake of celibacy and then must decide whether to land or not. Others may arrive at islands of celibacy on a lake of sexual activity, and they must decide to disembark or not and for how long.

Just as people differ in their needs for closeness and distance emotionally, they differ in their needs for sexual closeness or distance at any given time. If one is comfortable with one's sexuality but feels a declining interest in it, one must feel free to be celibate if desired. It would not always be good to continue having sex when one doesn't feel like having sex, no matter what social obligations may prevail. If sex has become unfulfilling but one continues to participate, it takes on a character of *unnaturalness.* That means that sex has become an inappropriate means of expression of the personality at that time. If people are expressing something other than what they are or less than what they are at any given moment, they will feel frustrated, less open, less full, diminished, cut off from their feelings.

The fuller levels of feeling, the deep levels of tenderness and intimacy, can easily be lost in sex because sexual activity is so dominating and tends to hold the focus of attention when people are making love. You may long to express these deeper parts to your lover but may end up expressing only the sexual. It is then that an individual or a couple may decide in favor of celibacy. It may not be a long period of celibacy—perhaps only a week or two—but it can be just what is needed at the time.

At the very least, celibacy can offer the opportunity for "refueling" sexuality. As pure unexpressed sexuality, the celibate state is the "rest state" of sexuality and, as such, contains the full potential of one's sexuality. But it also contains the full potential of all love experiences as well as other spiritual possibilities. It is in no way meant to deny love: on the contrary, it is meant to revitalize it and redis-cover it. As Richardson notes, "The renunciation of sexual activity is not a renunciation of love . . . rather of that kind of love that has sexual orgasm and procreation as its pur-pose."

Celibacy can offer an *alternative* approach to love and loving by allowing sexuality to remain at rest in its most delicate and unbounded state. By choosing to be celibate, we renew our sexuality while, at the same time, we find new and more subtle ways of expressing and feeling love.

To have new experiences in life, often we have to break certain rigid patterns of behavior in order to free ourselves to enjoy other possibilities that might be lying dormant. In *The Pleasure Areas*, H. J. Campbell points out that for our lives to grow freely, the pathways in the brain have to be newly reestablished:

> When information is processed by the brain, preferred path-ways are established. . . . Only brains that contain preferred pathways can exhibit the characteristics of a mind. . . . If the conditions are right, the same such pathways can be ob-literated in favor of new ones. . . .
>
> A person whose behavior is based upon indoctrinated pre-ferred pathways is no less a machine than the computer that behaves according to a preset program. . . . We can only

attain individuality, personal freedom and nonmechanical life if we determine our own preferred pathways.[10]

New neural response patterns are easy for us to establish. And we can establish new kinds of response in love, in creating, in perceiving, simply by being celibate.

If something is imposed from the outside, it can become a barrier. But if it is self-imposed—from inside—it can be a means to achievement. In a closed system of behavior, where patterning is fixed and rigid due to fear, anxiety, and psychophysical blocking, celibacy may appear pathological. In an open system of behavior, where the person has grown beyond the regular need pattern of a sexual commitment, celibacy may be evolutionary.

Tuning in to Nonsexual Responses

Just as silence is the basis for sound, for speech, for music, celibacy is the basis for sex. The quietness of the celibate state has the potential to give rise to active sexual functioning. Sexual expression can be very gross or very subtle, depending on the feelings and awareness of the individuals involved in the expression; celibacy can be understood in the context of sexuality as the subtlest form of sexuality—potential but unexpressed.

If a person has been playing the stereo constantly for weeks and then turns it off one day, he immediately "hears" the silence, and that silence seems full. Listening more closely, he may even hear in his own head some subtle music that is more charming than what he was listening to on the stereo all that time.

By being celibate, by turning off the "sexual stereo," one may discover a whole new dimension of response in love, in creation, in perception underneath the sexual program. People may then find that they are able to begin to experience a quality of attention that makes them more tuned in to feelings of intimacy, tenderness, and fullness of love in the relationship, as well as in other parts of their lives. Instead of being dominated by just one kind of human love response—the sexual—they are free to experience other responses.

Celibacy is a way of breaking boundaries, old patterns of behavior that exist between the mind and body, between the self and others. It enables one to be free of sexuality in order to evaluate and experience the joys of life without sex. If the results of being celibate for some time lead to becoming sexual once again, fine; it will be bringing about an even more sexually alive state than before. If one chooses to remain celibate because other nonsexual experiences turn out to be very fascinating, then too there will be clear benefits resulting from the celibate exploration.

The
Old Celibacy

2   CELIBACY IN RELIGION

The deepest insight from theology, I believe, is that men are
created for communion with God and the universality of
being, but that they cannot attain to this communion until
they have overcome their narcissistic love of self . . . and
are able to love all persons equally and fully. To overcome
narcissistic love, the disciplines of virginity and celibacy
have been—and will continue to be—essential spiritual disciplines.

—HERBERT RICHARDSON

The gift of celibacy is, in reality, the call to be a "seer," a
man of vision, a vision of his own dignity, a dedication to
others . . . loving inside a vast reality. This vision is necessary for a celibate to be a well-adjusted and happy person.

—JOSEPH WADE

In the life of the religious, celibacy has long been a spiritual
discipline, an exercise for the devotee to advance in
spiritual growth. It has been suggested that celibacy offers a
way for the religious individual to have his or her attention
most purely absorbed in the commitment to seeking and
experiencing God.

In the practices of various ancient religions, celibacy was sacerdotal—represented in the power of the shaman, the priests and the priestesses—wherein sexual power was ritually transformed into religious power. More generally, throughout history, those religious individuals dedicated to spiritual life set themselves apart from the larger society and male and female monasticism was established as a religious lifestyle. Celibacy was practiced to further spiritual goals and perform service to God in one-pointed, pure devotion. Typically, these devouts have lived cloistered in groups or solitary—like the hermit, the wandering ascetic, or the priest living a monastic life within the secular community.

The tradition of celibacy is established in about half the major world religions. Interestingly, the tradition breaks the usual division between Eastern and Western cultures. For example, celibacy is traditional in the Eastern religions of Hinduism, Buddhism, Taoism, and Jainism but not in Islam or Confucianism. Likewise, in the West, celibacy is traditional in Roman Catholicism and the Eastern Orthodox Church but not in Judaism or Protestantism.

Hinduism

Of all the world religions past and present, celibacy is most widely practiced in the Eastern religions, particularly in Hinduism. Just as one does not have to be a priest to lead a religious life within Hinduism, one does not have to be a priest to be celibate. The male and female celibate devotees, whether priests or not, are the *sadhus*—the "holy ones."

In the 5000-year-old Hindu tradition, the ideal spiritual life consists of four stages, representing four developmental behavioral stages of ideal human growth. One begins with the *bramacharya* (celibate) life of the young student. Around age ten, the *bramacharin* embarks upon a rigorous training in knowledge in which his celibate status serves as the basis for growing consciousness. He studies, usually with a master, while maintaining celibacy for the next twelve years. This training is followed by a second stage, *garhasthya*—the active daily life of marriage and family. Not all marry at this time; some continue as monks and remain celibate for their entire lives, but most marry and raise families. Both paths—that of the celibate and of the householder—are equally respected in Hinduism.

Of those who have married, some will continue to uphold the spiritual commitment to ideal life and choose to leave active life to become religious recluses during the third stage, *vanaprastha*. Some married couples go together to the forest or mountains, but as celibates, for this third stage is a return to celibate life. It is a time to be free of worldly possessions and family duties and continues into the last stage, *sanyasa*, which requires a life completely alone, the renunciation of all family and friends as well as all material things. The *sanyasin* enjoys silence through meditation and is committed to radiating the purity of his or her highly developed consciousness throughout the universe.

Buddhism

Out of the Hindu tradition of ideal spiritual life came the Buddha—Gautama Siddartha—who 2500 years ago founded the monastic order of Buddhism, which has since come to include both monks and married people. In modern Buddhism in Tibet, Japan, and Thailand, monks are permitted to marry. And married men may spend time as monks prior to and during the course of married life, alternating celibate life with marriage. But the most devout aspirants in the Buddhist tradition emphasize monasticism and long-term celibacy as a foundation of the contemplative life in order to achieve the state known as *arhat*—the state of enlightenment—through the establishment of complete freedom and detachment from material life, including the bonds of sexuality.

Tantric Tradition

A later Indian tradition, Tantra, came to hold that celibacy was not necessary for the growth of spiritual life. The basic teaching of Tantra is the unity of *nirvana* and *samsara*, the integration of mystical and sensual experience. And, in fact, no real difference is seen between the two. A two-in-one correlation creates the unity of two polar entities into one encompassing whole. These polar energies are most often symbolized in sexual terms. All spirituality in the Tantric tradition is considered based in sexuality: male and female are juxtaposed to create new unity with regard to knowledge, God, and enlightenment.

The Eastern traditions, particularly the Tantric, use the power of sexuality to express spirituality symbolically. In all the so-called erotic literature of the East, one misses the great meaning of the works if the ritual and symbolic content is ignored. By the same token, Eastern celibacy is not merely nonsexuality—nor is it associated with "nonsinfulness" for the sake of being "good" for God.

In the Eastern traditions, celibacy represents a discipline to gain enlightenment, whereby all the physical, mental, and emotional energy of the body, mind, and senses is directed toward progressively higher levels of evolution. The understanding is that to find God, one has to transcend the thought of God; to let the heart be fully opened to God, one has to transcend emotion. In the same way, to be fully spiritual, one becomes celibate—in order to transcend the boundaries of sex.

Western celibacy does not have a tradition of physical and spiritual growth associated with it the way the Eastern traditions do. And the Western outlook on celibacy varies considerably from religion to religion and also within each particular religion.

Judaism
The ancient tenets of Judaism embraced marriage for all, including the rabbis, who had to be married in order to pursue higher study. (One exception was the unmarried prophet Jeremiah.)

However, the rituals of Jewish marriage were such that sex was not in the least indiscriminate but very strictly disciplined. And, in some cases, in order to study the Torah and other Jewish scriptures, rabbis would ask permission from their wives to be celibate and free of familial concerns in order to devote themselves exclusively to knowledge. But, among the Jewish sects, there was one notable group, the Essenes—who appeared two centuries before Christ— who were known for being celibate.

The Essenes were an ascetic sect associated with the Qumran community from the region around the Dead Sea where the Qumran documents—the Dead Sea Scrolls— were written.

Like the Shakers centuries later, the Essenes were a community of celibates who believed in the control of the bodily passions for the purpose of cultivating a pure and holy nature. They lived simply, with emphasis on humility, obedience, and purity. They participated in none of the animal sacrifices common to the times. Unlike the Shakers, however, almost all were men. Apparently, although some were married and some celibate only temporarily, most were committed life celibates. They lived in a community of equal fellowship and were said to be intolerant of outsiders and not particularly friendly to women. According to the historian Pliny, the Essenes often participated in family life by adopting young children to raise.

Celibacy and Christianity

Celibacy in the Christian religion has been generally regarded not as a physical discipline to purify the body and enliven consciousness but as an exemplary virtue of devotion to God. Unfortunately, the tradition of celibacy in Christianity has suffered through a history of sexual misunderstanding without much benefit of the knowledge and experience of the value of celibacy to unfold the higher states of experience of God found in the Eastern religions.

For the most part, Christian celibacy has been utilized as an uneasy refuge for warding off the evils of sexuality, based on the belief in original sin. The Christian concept of original sin (traced to the female, notes historian Barbara Tuchman, "Theology being the work of males") holds that sexual knowledge and experience prevent one from entering the Kingdom of Heaven after death. So, in order for the individual to be accepted, sexuality must be rooted out—and that is most simply accomplished through abstaining from sexual activity.

But abstinence as a standard of religious devotion hasn't had much success in the 2000 years it has been upheld as an ideal in Christianity.

The issues of celibacy and sex were initially separate from the Christian religion. They were introduced in the belief that with the advent of the New Age heralded by the coming of Christ, the Kingdom of God was at hand and there would be no need for marriage since, in St. Paul's view, "all would be like angels." Jesus was said to have encouraged the single celibate life for his disciples: "Let those accept it who can." Some apostles, like Peter, married but others gave up married life and family responsibilities to devote themselves to the "New Age." A favoring of the single life over married life for the religious came to predominate and eventually marriage, in its association with sex, became something less than fully spiritual in Christianity. As St. Paul wrote in the *First Epistle to the Corinthians*:

> I would that all men were even as I myself [i.e., celibate]. . . . I say, therefore, to the unmarried and widows, it is good for them if they thus abide even as I. But if they cannot contain, let them marry: for it is better to marry than to burn.

St. Paul, according to Bertrand Russell, saw marriage as the lesser evil when compared with indiscriminate sex. "The Christian view that all intercourse outside marriage is immoral was . . . based upon the view that all sexual intercourse, even within marriage, is regrettable . . . and something of a handicap in the attempt to win salvation."

Priest Donald Goergen maintains that the "sin" of sexuality as the enemy of spirituality began with Paul and was magnified by Augustine. Augustine encouraged celibacy in marriage. For him "chastity can be celibate or conjugal, and conjugal chastity is still true chastity. Conjugal chastity limits sexual intercourse quite explicitly to procreation." Tuchman also emphasizes Augustine's abhorrence of sexuality for its own sake. "Using copulation for the delight that is in it and not for the end intended was, Augustine ruled, a sin against nature and, therefore, against God. . . . Celibacy and virginity remained preferred states because they allowed total love of God, 'the spouse of the soul.' "[1]

Augustine would have adored the advent of test-tube babies. In his dilemma over how to reconcile procreation and sex, he wrote: "They who marry wives for this purpose only [procreation], if the means could be given them of having children without intercourse with their wives, would they not with joy unspeakable embrace so great a blessing?"

It is no surprise that historian D. S. Bailey concludes: "Augustine must bear no small measure of responsibility for the insinuation into our culture of the idea still widely current, that Christianity regards sexuality as something peculiarly tainted with evil."

British historian W. E. H. Lecky, in his *History of European Morals,* also observed that marriage was degraded by the early Christians as an inferior state. Although necessary for the propagation of the species, it was considered a necessary evil. But for an individual wanting to maintain the commitment to a Christian life, marriage was more than a compromise; it was nearly a contract of sin. How could one continue to have sex—the "orginal sin"—*and* aspire to a sin-free life?

St. Bernard used to preach the gospel of marital celibacy so persuasively on street corners in various villages that all the careful wives would hide their husbands when he was in town. Lecky cites various saints who resolved the sexual-marriage–versus–devout-Christian contradiction by leaving their marriages entirely.

The separation between marriage and the priesthood

did not begin formally until 305 A.D., when the Spanish Council of Elvira decreed that all married clergy were to abstain from sex with their wives. Up until that time, the clergy married and could maintain sexual lives. So celibate marriage among the clergy was presumably practiced for eight centuries, until the First Lateran Council in 1123 A.D. prohibited marriage for priests. Only toward the end of the thirteenth century was the celibacy of the clergy rigidly enforced.

When Christianity began to branch out into various new sects, the practice of celibacy for the clergy became reserved primarily for Roman Catholicism and Eastern Orthodoxy. And although occasionally recommended, it disappeared almost entirely from the lives of the Protestant clergy. Both John Calvin and Martin Luther upheld the values of celibacy but did not insist on it. As Luther said: "A preacher of the Gospel, if he is able with a good conscience to remain unmarried, let him so remain; but if he cannot abstain, living chastely, then let him take a wife. God has made this plaster for that sore."

As sexuality became more acceptable in Christianity over the centuries, celibacy took on a more rarefied air. Practicing celibates grew further and further apart from the larger society. Celibacy for most Christians continued to be understood as the opposite of sexuality. One was either sexual *or* celibate. And as sexuality became more "natural," celibacy seemed to become more "unnatural." Today, celibacy has become a major issue in the church—praised by the few and maligned by the many.

Modern Monastic Celibacy:
Sexual versus Sexless

In an article on being a nun in America, Sister M. Roberta tells the story of her aunt, also a nun, a woman in her sixties. The aunt was riding on a train across from another woman who kept glaring at her during the ride. Finally, unable to hide her disgust any longer, the woman turned on her and practically shouted, "What's the matter with you girls? Can't you get a man?"

As of the early 1970s, there were an estimated 59,000 priests, 160,000 nuns, and 12,000 monks in the U.S.— figures said to be on the decrease. This may be due in part to the way that priests, nuns, and monks are treated in our "sexually liberated" society. Their lives are often evaluated as unnatural rather than understood as spiritual, primarily because so little in our society upholds the possibility of growth through spiritualized sexuality. Joseph Wade, a priest who conducted research on modern religious life, concluded that the life of the religious celibate is seen by others as a life of frustration. Those committed to a religious vocation are judged to be "frustrated in their human desires, trapped in a detested form of life . . . and forced into close, uncongenial contacts."

Whereas celibates throughout the ages have been regarded at least as uplifting examples of the spiritual development of human life, suggesting the possibility of a life directed to more than worldly ends, today religious celibates are no longer given the respect and admiration they received earlier.

As a result, religious devouts may experience undue prejudice against their commitment from the community, based on such concerns as "How can a celibate understand?" And, according to Wade, they may actually be grieved over by their families. Without much support from the rest of society for their chosen life, some modern monastics experience a kind of personal alienation that can be devastating.

Besides societal prejudice, there are other psychological reasons why monastic life has been found to be so difficult today. Priest Paul Conner explains:

> A comparison of pre-modern times with ours reveals that earlier peoples developed more naturally and stably at home in their human relationships. . . . Their simpler familial and

agrarian society favored this, which explains in large part why many men and women of those times were able to live contented lives in the monastic setting. In our technological epoch . . . never having sufficient human love as children and adolescents, they thirst for it as adults. This is, perhaps, an underlying reason why few committed Christians today seem able to live contentedly within the confines of strict monastic communities.[2]

Similarly, Wade observed an overall lack of understanding of how to deal with sexuality among the monastics he studied, but he found that those from loving homes were better adjusted to celibacy. Those with affectionate parents had much less difficulty accepting their own sexuality, and therefore their celibacy, than did those who came from homes where there was little affection or sex education. He found that where there had been a lack of love in the home, by age thirty and over, a mental change often takes place— an awareness on the part of the priest that he is not fulfilled in love.

And where there has been a lack of integration and naturalness, priests report feeling the lack of intimacy and may experience what Wade describes as an emotional coldness. According to Goergen, celibacy may bring loneliness to the monastic life not because of sexual needs but by ignoring the more basic need for intimacy and closeness to others. So, despite their religious commitment, some priests may not be ready for celibacy either physiologically or psychologically. The years of denial may be overwhelming, especially if attention is constantly going toward sexuality. One often attends with great interest to that which one thinks one cannot have. So whereas for some priests celibacy is natural and comfortable, for others it is not. And when an unnatural celibacy is compounded by a lack of close friendships and little experience of love, it is no wonder that a priest may choose rather "to marry than to burn."

This perhaps explains in part why a decade ago, the

Ficter survey researching the outlook and opinions of modern Catholic priests reported that two out of three priests wanted to be permitted to marry and favored voluntary over dogmatic celibacy, saying that optional celibacy would be better than enforced celibacy within the Church.

Despite the protest, in the spring of 1979, Pope John Paul II upheld mandatory celibacy for Roman Catholic priests and nuns and reminded them that Jesus referred to the celibate state "as a gift for the Kingdom of Heaven." The Pope pointed out that no one is forced to take celibate vows and that the priests must not give in to the various forms of manipulation that they meet.

And there are many priests, nuns, and monks who have confronted and accepted their sexual natures so completely that they are happily and comfortably celibate. A thirty-four-year-old Catholic priest interviewed by the author had this to say about celibacy:

> Celibacy is a very simple thing to me. I have learned to deal with sexuality by simply accepting it and not trying to avoid it as a reality of life. I don't think that being celibate means refusing love. I am by nature a friendly and outgoing fellow and I've shared and will continue to share many happy and joyous times with my family and dear friends during my life—I am, after all, Italian. And through these relationships, I feel my love for God deepen immeasurably. But it is God whom I serve above all. I think you will find that those of us who maintain celibacy in the service of God do not exclude love from our lives but rather seek to uphold its value everywhere, in all our interactions with the world.

SECULAR CELIBACY

In Eastern history, religious and secular life have been much more intertwined than in the West; consequently, the polarization of sexuality versus celibacy or marriage versus spiritual life has not occurred with the same intensity as in Western history. In the East, sexuality and celibacy are

considered two expressions of the same energy phenomenon.

In general, sex in the East represents the spending of
energy, and celibacy its conservation. Excessive sexual
interest is not considered a sin but rather a weakness, an
unnecessary waste of mental and physical energy, whereas
celibacy represents mental and physical strength through
the conserving of energy. It is recognized that sex is the
basis of celibacy and celibacy the basis of sex. But one has
to be sexually ready to be celibate. One accepts one's sexuality, and then, if physiology permits, proceeds to its more
refined values in the celibate state.

There are those in the East who have wrongly advocated celibacy as the ideal means of birth control for whole
nations, regardless of the sexual and spiritual readiness of
individuals to practice it, leading to unfortunate results in
overpopulation. But when practiced by those for whom it is
sexually timely and useful, celibacy has been generally respected as a means of personal growth throughout the history of Eastern life.

Not so in the West. Here, the practice of celibacy in
secular life has had a confused and fragmented history.
There have been no large movements to celibate life, nor
have any major societies embraced celibacy as a secular
spiritual discipline. Rather, at its best, celibacy has been an
experiment for certain individuals and communities seeking
ways to bring about self-fulfillment and/or social change. At
its worst, celibacy has been misused as a means of severe
repression to uphold an antisexual position.

In a civilization where sex has been, for the most part,
a heavily charged (mostly negative) issue, celibacy has also
been a charged issue—sometimes revered and sometimes
reviled—based not on its developmental usefulness but on its
seemingly antisexual nature. Of course, as psychologist Joe
K. Adams suggests, "There is good reason to believe that
the sex taboos in Western civilization have never prevented
or even minimized the forbidden sexual activities them-

selves."[3] And there is also good reason to believe that the practice of celibacy was never widely accepted beyond its theoretical virtuousness. Where it had been practiced, celibacy in the West had often been "unnatural" and caused great suffering; and where it had been abandoned completely, its loss had also caused great suffering.

In ancient Greece, celibacy was often actually treated as a crime. For example, at one time the city of Sparta denied the rights of citizenship to unmarried men. But around the same era, in 529 B.C., the mathematician Pythagoras established a small community at Croton in South Italy to study and practice sexual abstinence and vegetarianism. And, of course, the most famous secular formulation of celibate love—Platonic love—was created in this culture in Plato's "ideal society." In this society, human love transcends its sexual limitations and becomes a quest for the Ideal of love—an eternal, nonchanging basis for all experiences of fulfillment in love. Love is considered the basis for union, sex but an unnecessary diversion. Platonic love is described as a powerful means of coming to experience the unity or wholeness of life, which is far beyond the sexual. In this way, celibacy allows the self in love to rise to another plane of reality.

Later on, in the first century A.D., the philosopher Apollonius of Tyana espoused celibate living for his disciples to aid detachment and equilibrium in thought. Similarly, the Stoics of the Roman Empire, who replaced the sensual Epicureans, favored the discipline of celibacy. In 50 A.D., for example, the Stoic philosopher Epictetus taught that celibacy would calm the philosopher, balance his body and mind, and free him from distracting family cares.

Then there were the famed Vestal Virgins of ancient Rome. During their requisite thirty years of service, celibacy was, of course, maintained, but even after the service was ended, many of the women chose to remain celibate and single throughout the rest of their lives.

During the early days of Christianity, writes Herbert

Richardson, in *Nun, Witch, Playmate,* marriage was considered quite unholy because it allowed sexual activity even if only for procreation. Thus, "the commitment to permanent virginity as the basis for a truly spiritual marriage became a not uncommon practice." According to historian D. S. Bailey, this phenomenon of spiritual marriage in secular life was called *syneisaktism* and was "a co-habitation of the sexes under conditions of strict continence, a couple sharing the same house, often the same room, and sometimes even the same bed, yet conducting themselves as brother and sister."

During the Middle Ages and later, it was the laity or secular society who were said to have introduced the concept of spiritualized love between men and women (which included the celibate practices for men discussed in a later chapter). It was called courtly or romantic love and was thought of as the secular attempt to personalize the feelings associated with the love of God.

At that time, the love of God had become a somewhat distant, depersonalized experience, almost completely associated with the church alone. As the churches grew vaster and their spires higher in the seeming attempt to touch God in heaven, the desire to share devotional love with someone on a more intimate, more human scale was structured into the procedures of courtly or romantic love.

It was the first time that personal conversation and communication occurred between the sexes. And, according to Herbert Richardson, courtly love extended the sexual process to include a number of "symbolic-affective" steps, each an end in itself. Different steps were taken for different relationships—a romantic conversation, a kiss, or more physical behavior, depending on the situation. It was, no doubt, the forerunner of our "step-by-step" dating procedure, but the steps were not goal-oriented. Rather, they were expressions of the value of a particular relationship. It was, says Richardson, a specific voluntary control over sexual behavior to gain the rewards of intimacy. It ultimately permitted all forms of sexuality "excepting orgasm"—orgasm being involuntary and unintentional and thus considered nonpersonal in expression. As Richardson concludes, "To make sex an expression of love requires a learning process. The courtly lovers abstained, therefore, from all those aspects of sexual interaction that they could not bring within the range of personal intention and voluntary control."

Courtly love eventually lost its appeal. Later on, when the love relationships between men and women were commonly accepted as primarily physical, the regulations of courtly love were laughed at as restrictive and unnatural. Shakespeare, the Romantics, and Freud were among its critics. But only seeing it as sexually repressive, they failed to recognize how freely it allowed love to grow.

Courtly love, perhaps *because* of its conscious rules, ennobled the ideal of love in very personal human relationships, yet it never allowed the lovers to become overshadowed in their expression of love. It was never false or overblown: devotional love grew in accordance with the consciousness of the lovers who maintained full awareness of every act and chose each act of love for the accuracy of its expression. What it lacked in spontaneity it made up for in clarity. It was not confusing or disorderly; it allowed for balanced growth of all parts of the personality in the cause of loving. Moreover, it stands as perhaps the best example in Western history of the use of celibacy in the service of growth through love.

Throughout the centuries to come, as sexuality became negatively repressed instead of positively controlled, the "sinful" character of sex would often so dominate human relations that personal love too would become degraded and no longer regarded as an appropriate channel for the development of human life. We can speculate that this is where celibacy got the bad reputation it has today, when it became falsely associated with sexual repression rather than with love.

This situation came about many times in Western history—as sin and sex were many times confused. As Barbara Tuchman concisely remarked, "Of all mankind's ideas, the equating of sex with sin has left the greatest train of trouble." And if, as Donald Goergen observed, we identify sexual desire as sinful, "repression is almost inevitable." And a time of sexual repression was never more clearly in evidence in Western history than in America.

The Puritans

Starting with the Puritans, America began its amazing history of sexual repression. In the seventeenth century, the Puritans used religion as the watchdog of sexual activity, and Christianity continued its history of what one scholar calls "sex-centered ideology."

The dour *New England Primer* opened with the famous couplet:

> In Adam's Fall
> We sinned all.

So as the Puritan child begins to read and starts with the first letter of the alphabet, the first concept he learns is that of original sin. Yet there was no secrecy about sex for the Puritans. They were realists, says historian Milton Rugoff, "only too well-aware of the hungers of the body." They had no faith in voluntary celibacy but believed that sexual desires—"the most subversive of total devotion to God"—could only be suppressed by fear-induced continence based on wrath and denunciation. They didn't deny sexuality shyly, they denounced it vociferously.

But by the nineteenth century, sexuality had become so repressed as to be almost invisible. No longer a hellfire-and-damnation religious issue, it had become an internalized conflict—a psychological and moral issue and a breeding ground for our modern rebellion.

America was the land of freedom and expansion in almost every area except the sexual. Even while Americans were settling a continent and constantly experimenting with new methods and innovative solutions, sexuality was taboo, considered totally shameful, and narrow rules for sex were rigidly adhered to. But, says Rugoff, there is "a law of sexual dynamics: repression eventually breeds evasion or rebellion." And both these reactions occurred in America's sexual history.

Lacking any real knowledge of the realities of sexuality, nineteenth-century Americans focused heavily upon its mysteries and progressed in a peculiarly American way in two different sexual directions—some toward further self-denial, which became "quiet evasion" in the conforming lives of the Victorians, and some toward an increased freedom of sexual expression in the experimental communities of the latter part of the century. Celibacy was prescribed in both cases—but in one its use was wholly negative and in the other quite sophisticated and positive.

The Victorians

Whereas the Puritans had waged great, loud battles to suppress sexuality, the Victorians were so horrified by sex that they completely denied its existence. The Victorian ideal was the total sublimation of sex—"nothing showing." It wasn't discussed, but it was certainly implied. The outer appearances of propriety were valued far more than any hidden realities. But under the surface of respectability, prostitution and abortion were practiced everywhere.

In family life, sexual love was seen as degrading—"for the beasts only." Men were acknowledged to have sexual desires but were supposed to refrain from imposing them on their wives. They tried cold showers, exercise, hard beds, religious prayer and, eventually, prostitutes. The concept of propriety in marriage overtook all normal feelings of love and became an intense kind of prudery, not a striving for purity. Wives, however, were not even supposed to have sexual desires at all and were taught to participate in procreative sexual activity only for the benefit of their spouses and families. Thus they led virtually celibate lives. (Not that any aspect of women's physical makeup could have been known: the prudery of the times was so great that female cadavers could not even be dissected in the medical schools.)

But the Victorians' attempt to eradicate their sexuality was to no avail. By attempting to negate eroticism, everything became eroticized. A glance, an uncovered ankle, a blushing cheek all took on special sexual significance in the absence of other possibilities. So the time and energy spent in the interior lives of the Victorians on sexualized thinking—not only in America, but in England and the "more civilized" parts of Europe as well—turned out to be much greater than in many less repressive eras.*

Not until the beginning of this century did a lifting of these self-imposed sexual sanctions begin to occur, partly under the mutually reinforcing influences of the advent of birth control and the public awareness of the theories of Freud and his contemporaries. Central to the new thinking on sexuality was the idea that sexuality is neither criminal, sinful, nor abnormal.

And eventually, relatively "sin-free" sex began to take on the aura of actual enjoyment, even though it was "enjoyed" very seriously. The experts of the day began to "prescribe" it, following Freud's admonition that sexual repression caused neuroses and untold physical ailments. Then came the theory that celibacy was actually harmful

*Despite the influence of Freud, not every authority considers the sexual restrictiveness of the nineteenth century to be entirely negative. At least one eminent historian, Arnold Toynbee, concludes that the denial of sexuality represented the overcoming of biological boundaries and became an important contributing factor in the century's great creative expansion. He wrote: "I admire the nineteenth century West's success in postponing the age of sexual awakening, sexual experience and sexual infatuation far beyond the age of physical puberty. You may tell me that this was against nature; but to be human consists precisely in transcending nature—in overcoming the biological limitations that we have inherited from our pre-human ancestors." ("Why I Dislike Western Civilization," *The New York Times Magazine*, May 10, 1964) because the reproductive organs would grow weak if not used regularly. This idea was then soundly protested by such physicians as Dr. Arthur Gould, who argued in 1906, "If that were true, the boy who exercises his sexuality regularly from youth onward should have the greatest sexual strength—but the reverse is true. Sexual power is never lost through abstinence, as the ability to weep is not lost through not weeping."

According to Gould, semen is secreted and redistributed throughout the body to nourish brain, muscles, bones, and sinews. He considered "spermatazoa the most highly vitalized form of living matter . . . the most precious nutriment of the blood. . . . Overproduction of semen from either thought or practice is a serious strain and waste of vitality."

The idea of sexual waste of valuable energy and youth was a direct steal from the East but was echoed by a number of Westerners in the first decades of this century. And Bertrand Russell and others concluded that not only were the physical strains of sex excessive, but the mental and social attention put on things sexual also were excessive and, ultimately, dangerous.

At the same time that Victorian America was furtively covering and uncovering ankles, a small group of Americans began to seek new ways to live together, free of self-deception and pretension. Thus, in the mid-nineteenth century, a number of structured communities were founded to promote a social concept or purpose for ideal community life. These communities attracted what Rugoff calls the "spiritual avant-garde of the period"—young people who were seeking ways to satisfy their spiritual longings and "Puritan monks, who rejected the world and saw celibacy and labor as a loftier, more spiritual way of life."

Among these societies were those experimenting in "free love," but, interestingly, some form of celibacy often formed the basis for the sexual freedom. And other experimental communities were exclusively celibate.

Herbert Richardson compares these American utopian societies of the nineteenth century with the monastic traditions which emerged during medieval times—wherein the communities, by "renouncing sexual intercourse and raising celibacy to an ideal," were reorienting sexual desire to a new form of expression—the spiritual "communalization" of sex.

The most famous of the secular American celibates were (and still are) the Shakers. The Shaker community, founded near Albany, New York, was a close-knit society of men and women which was aimed at "perfect simplicity." The words of their well-known song perhaps best illustrate their outlook:

> Tis the gift to be simple—
> Tis the gift to be free—
> Tis the gift to come down where we ought to be.
> And when we find ourselves in the place just right—
> Twill be in the valley of love and delight.
> When true simplicity is gained,
> To bow and to bend—we shan't be ashamed.
> To turn and to turn
> Will be our delight
> 'Till by turning, turning, we come round right.

The "turning" no doubt refers, at least in part, to the ritual "dance" all Shakers performed before retiring to bed each evening. Most interpreters of this "whirling" activity see it as a technique the Shakers used to "neutralize the desire for coition" or as a release of sexual tension. The "dance" is also often considered to be orgasmic—a form of communal sex growing from the renunciation of genital sex and leading to what Richardson calls "a new polymorphous total sexuality." But there are also other dimensions of the "turning-around" ritual to consider.

When one whirls around continuously, the outer external cues one generally relies upon for locating oneself in space tend to disappear and one may experience a moment of unboundedness, free of outward boundaries. So this Shaker ritual can also be understood as a technique for free-

ing oneself from physical limitations, if only temporarily—
where reliance on inner cues is called for—in order to "come
round right." One thus becomes momentarily self-reliant,
free from the field of external information.

The Shaker "dance" may also be deeply symbolic and
spiritual in intent and effect: a way to "shake off" pride,
egotism, shame, or any of the human weaknesses that disal-
low the experience of "true simplicity" and deep
humility—the simplest form of the self, free from all personality restrictions—"'Till by turning, turning, we come
round right."

The Shakers led the exemplary life of pure monasticism. All arose and retired at the same time: everyone dined
together in silence. No stimulants such as coffee, tea, alcohol, or tobacco were permitted, and disease was considered
a "sin against God." The Shakers understood God to have
both male and female characteristics and saw the purpose
of union to be union *within* the individual, not just union
between two individuals. So remaining celibate for them
was a way to be like God.

Despite, or perhaps because of, their impressive self-
discipline, the Shakers were observed to be warm and affectionate with each other. Although men and women were not
allowed to talk together privately, all shared a common
purpose and a common communication possibly reaching
far deeper than words. All maintained celibacy, even the
married couples who joined.

The communal efforts of the Shakers in material pro-
duction were very successful; they structured an environment of purposefulness and creativity and became well
known as great inventors and innovators. (One familiar area
of Shaker design—furniture-making—produced some of the
most beautiful pieces ever made in America.) Yet, even at
their peak of productivity, in 1860, there were only 6000
members. Since no children are born in the community,
membership is only maintained if new people join. By 1900
the membership had decreased to 1000, and today there are
only small groups of Shakers. (During the 1960s, some

members of the counterculture tried to join the Shaker community but did not last long, apparently unable to keep up with the disciplined pace of Shaker life.)

Other celibate communities of nineteenth-century America included the Rappites of New Harmony, Indiana, and (later) Economy, Pennsylvania. The 800-member society was founded by a German industrialist less for the purpose of spiritual living than for economic reasons. The Rappites were willing to forego sex in order to secure freedom from financial want. Like the Shakers, their work productivity was enormous and of the highest quality, and they grew to be a very wealthy community. All were celibate, but in the interests of maintaining economic growth, married couples were allowed to live together for procreative purposes one year out of seven.

Another midcentury community was the Memnonia Society, founded in Yellow Springs, Ohio. This was a community advancing not work productivity but the social experiment of "free love." Its small membership paid to join, much as one would at a vacation resort or health spa. A ninety-day celibacy was required before sexual union between any of the members was allowed. This was structured in order for the experience of sexual union to be given time to grow in the qualities of spiritual union as well. Besides celibacy, certain Eastern techniques of lovemaking were practiced along with vegetarianism and water fasts—all activities geared to creating more heightened experiences in the "experiment" of loving.

In 1872, the Oneida Colony—the most bold and successful of all the nineteenth-century experimental communities—was founded by John Noyes in Oneida, New York. It lasted thirty years and drew hundreds of participants. It too was a love-oriented rather than work-oriented communal experiment. Although not a celibate community, the Oneida Colony is classified with the others because of its commitment to exploration beyond the sexual level of love. The emphasis was on self-control and mental enjoyment of love between members and no one participated in indiscriminate sexuality. Noyes contended that his teachings on sexual practice had more in common with Shaker celibacy than with rampant free sexuality. The participants were given techniques to develop the heart and the spiritual possibilities of love. Under these circumstances, even multiple marriages were permitted.

The members of the Oneida community were taught by Noyes to distinguish between the "amative" and the "pro-creative" functions in lovemaking and to determine when each should be used according to its correct need. In amative love, male ejaculation was prohibited, in order, said Noyes, to make possible "the highest bliss of sexual fellowship for any length of time." Oneida became well known for the practice of this technique of male continence, which was used to teach maximum self-control as well as to allow the prolonged enjoyment of what Noyes described as "the sweetest and noblest period of intercourse . . . that first moment of simple presence and spiritual effusion before the muscular exercise begins." But the male also learned not to ejaculate because Noyes considered it "a wasteful expenditure of the seed and, therefore, unnatural."

Noyes advocated the same technique that Roman Catholics call *coitus reservatus* and that the Indian Tantric texts recommend for optimal male pleasure. Researcher Shere Hite refers to the revival of this technique today by experimenting male groups. Alfred C. Kinsey described its results as follows:

> In this technique it is common for the individual to experience as many as a dozen or twenty peaks of response which, while closely approaching the sexual climax, deliberately avoid what we should interpret as actual orgasm. Persons who practice such techniques commonly insist that they experience orgasm at each and every peak even though each is held to something below full response and . . . ejaculation is avoided.[4]

This technique was practiced at Oneida until children were desired and then the procreative function was employed.

In all these communities, whether truly celibate or not, the control or refinement of sexuality in a knowledge-able and positive way obviously distinguished them from the larger society where sex continued to be thought of as bad and worthy of revulsion only. In none of the small societies, not even among the Shakers, was sexuality de-graded; it was merely unattended to in the face of other goals considered more important for the community. Like the Eastern cultures which served at times as the models for these nineteenth-century communal enterprises, celibacy was a discipline for the purpose of human development, not for the purpose of ridding oneself of sexuality.

Modern Celibacy in Community: The Joy of Sects

In his book on new monastic communities, Charles Frac-chia describes a growing trend toward monastic life in the United States paralleling the recent religious reawakening. The new monastics are emerging from the fifty million un-married adults in this country, all searching, says Fracchia, for a life in a community. These spiritual enterprises are springing up not only in the deserts and mountains but also in the middle of large cities.

The emphasis, while definitely spiritual, is also familial—the sense of being part of a family is equally as im-portant as the religious rites practiced. Living with this mutual support, the new community participants say they can more easily live a religious life free from some of its harsher realities such as loneliness and economic depriva-tion, often made more harsh in modern times.

Some of these communities are following in the footsteps of the Shakers and the other nineteenth-century work communities and have developed very successful cot-tage industries in order to be self-sufficient and independent from the larger society. They bake bread, preserve fruits, sell weaving, pottery, and other commercial products. They work not only for economic purposes but "to experience God in the simplest tasks of daily living."

All faiths are represented in these communities but not necessarily along the old religious lines. For example, many Jewish and Catholic men and women were found to be participating in the Eastern spiritual communities—some even becoming priests and nuns within their new orders—and a number of non-Christians are turning toward the new Christianity. But the emphasis is often on regaining the "true" nature of the religious enterprise as formulated not twenty years ago but 2000 years ago, when the focus was on the idea of community in religious life.

The spiritual commitment of the new monastics is to personal growth, not simply to the dogmatized or ritualized aspects of religion. In this way, no real distinctions between the priest and the lay person are upheld—the common bonds of spiritual life are what bring these people together.

While the official church worries about the indifference of the laity, these young people are embracing monastic lifestyles that adhere to an even more rigorous morality than the church itself advocates. And in these societies, celibacy is often mandatory or at least desirable. The members learn to love each other "in community," as helpmates but not sexual mates.

One such community is Weston Priory in Vermont, where 700 to 1000 city people come on weekends to participate in the spiritual life of the monastery. Like the Shakers, the monks of Weston Priory use dance to celebrate prayer and worship.

Then there are the Eastern communities such as the Buddhist Orthodox group in northern California where men and women live separately and celibately. There are also modern Christian groups, such as the Holy Order of MANS—a nondenominational mystic organization that requires celibacy for its membership even during the year preceding the formal commitment.

At a solar-heated Benedictine monastery in New Mexico, single men and women—both secular and religious—live together but are celibate. One monk living there described the community: "We've all found that the importance of interaction between men and women in this community—and, mind you, we are all vowed to celibacy, even those who are in temporary commitment . . . is of inestimable value. The men and women complement each other."

The members are each assigned a "prayer partner" of the opposite sex. "We become very close to each other—like brother and sister—sharing each other's thoughts and feelings, ministering to each other. We are celibate, but we love one another. You know, I think this is a great preparation for marriage."

One nun comments on her experience:

> I lived in a community of women for more than twenty years, and I must honestly say that I far prefer a mixed community. . . . My own experience and that of people in the community here attest to the fact that you can have a celibate community composed of both men and women. Also, certain negative aspects of communities, either of all men or all women are lessened in a mixed community. The women become less petty and the men become softer.[5]

These new communities are essentially looking to establish a revival of spiritual life integrated with personal development. Celibacy offers the participants a new and perhaps deeper look at love. The "spiritualization" of life is based on the understanding and experience of the growth of nonsexual love—a concept that will be examined in the next chapter.

Celibacy and Love:
Does abstinence make the heart grow fonder?

THE LOVE TABOO: WHAT AND WHY

The inability to love fully and comfortably is one of the major problems of modern times. The big taboo today, according to several authorities, is not on sex, it's on love. Where people used to be afraid to express themselves sexually, now they are afraid to express themselves emotionally, particularly through the positive emotions of love and tenderness. As a result, writes Joe Adams, "Many people, perhaps most, are love-starved even more than they are sex-starved. . . ."

In our society, a young person quickly learns that sex is a more important accomplishment than love. And as the more subtle feelings of love become dominated by the more valued feelings of sexuality, eventually the love response becomes more difficult to stimulate—especially apart from the sexual response. Many therapists are finding that a growing number of the people they treat have to relearn how to love independently from sex. Essentially, they have to be instructed in what love comprises without constant reliance on accompanying sexual desires.

We've all been well taught that sexual attraction can be experienced separate from love—but somehow we've been coerced into believing that love apart from sex doesn't exist or, if it does exist, it doesn't mean much. We forget that in most relationships, the sexual aspect is neither the most important nor the most common ground for relating. One can relate nonsexually to everyone. We relate sexually only to a very few. And if a person finds that he or she must relate sexually to everyone, it is usually due to a pathological distortion of the personality. It is likely that, by trying to meet the need for love primarily through sexual activity, some people in our society have been "educated" or have trained themselves to exclude all other feelings of love in favor of the sexual ones. And this training may be starting at an early age.

Up until now, children have been observed to be most open to nonsexual loving because habits to express love sexually have not yet been fully ritualized in them. In his essay on love, Adams notes that children are able to love far more often and more easily than adults. He concludes that in terms of availability of impulses and feelings, "the average middle-aged person is quite dead" when compared with a healthy lively child. He explains that this happens because when an impulse or feeling cannot be expressed appropriately it will "gradually disappear or be transformed in some other impulse or feeling."

But children today often try to be sexual in an adult way before their bodies are ready to be so. Once they learn how to "act" sexual, they behave sexually more by mimicking what they have learned from the adult culture than by playing in a genuinely childlike sexual way. In the push to educate children in sexual matters, education in matter of loving is all but ignored. It is strange to consider that in the endless controversy over sex education in the schools, the issue hardly ever arises whether sex is even an appropriate thing to teach apart from an education in love. If children were taught all the ways there are to love, then sex would be taught as one possible way to express this most basic human need.

Children learn to love by being loved from birth on. It

is as essential as food. No one has ever died from a lack of sex, no matter how unfortunate they may feel, but research on infant needs conducted by René Spitz, Harry Harlow, John Bowlby, and others has demonstrated that without love, expressed in physical tenderness and cuddling, infant mortality rates go up significantly.

One of the major symptoms of our national avoidance of love and the nonsexual expression of feelings is the unwillingness to be physically close to and actually touch other people. Such avoidance would be understandable in a culture where sex was very much repressed, but in our culture it is often considered more inappropriate to touch others nonsexually than to have sex with them! This is because we generally don't touch other people *unless* we are going to have sex with them. This taboo on "interpersonal tactility," on touching—is, says Ashley Montagu, at least as great as the sexual taboo has been through the ages, both having arisen, he surmises, from the Christian church. But where we seem to have overcome the sexual taboo, we have not yet overcome the touch taboo.

As a matter of fact, we Americans are notorious for having created a "no-touch" culture. Sex is one of the only ways we allow ourselves to touch and be touched. Often the desire to be touched gets confused with the desire to have sex, when all one really wants is a little body contact of the mildest sort.

Human behavior experts have found that touching is one of the most basic indications of love and lack of hostility. Yet many people are deprived of the touch experience—both giving and receiving—to such an extent that they do not learn how to express emotion through touch. This deprivation is said to extend from childhood on and, not surprisingly, is found to be a specific problem related to sexual dysfunction. At their Reproductive Biology Research Institute in St. Louis, sexual researchers Masters and Johnson have spent a great deal of their therapeutic time teaching their dysfunctional patients how to express themselves simply through touching by a technique they call "sensate focusing." By teaching clients to focus on the sense of touch and on all the senses, Masters and Johnson use this more basic human response to help develop the sexual response. This has been found to be the right procedure to retrace the developmental behavioral sequence of learned inhibition from as early a stage as infancy where the baby and later the child learns "not to touch."

Masters and Johnson and other sex therapists may see the more extreme cases where fear of touching has contributed to the socially more disturbing phenomenon of sexual dysfunction. But there are many people who can function well sexually and still not touch. This is the symptom not of sexual dysfunction but of "intimacy dysfunction."

Intimacy is one of the most desired yet one of the most threatening of human experiences. It may be difficult for us to be intimate, but it is, after all, the intimacy that we long for in relationships, the intimacy that we value above all else. Rollo May pinpoints this longing when he writes that in remembering sexual experiences, it is the intimacy that is remembered, not the orgasm.

According to most psychologists, the reason we are afraid of being intimate, of allowing another person to get close to us emotionally, is because most of us are concerned that when our loved ones see us as we "really are," they will discover how shallow and inadequate we are "underneath." And so, the repudiation of intimacy is said to be based on feelings of unworthiness and a lack of confidence in oneself. To preserve a vivid love experience, one may feel compelled to push the lover away in order to avoid any resulting depreciation, rebuffs, frustration, dependency, or any other experience that one feels may burst the bubble of love for good.

Of course no one likes to be overshadowed by another or to feel that he or she will be judged inadequate. The fear of losing oneself in the relationship is a very valid fear. But such a fear will never be overcome unless one allows oneself to experience the depths of one's own feelings. Until a person knows on his own through his own understanding of himself that he is a truly worthy person, no one else can convince him of that worthiness. Many can try, but always there will be that self-doubt, the fear of being discovered as a sham, that will continue to inhibit the willingness to grow in any relationship. When this growth is disallowed, a lack of intimacy develops, and the result is loneliness—even within a longtime marriage.

Many psychologists and psychotherapists, including Harry Stack Sullivan, Erik Erikson, Abraham Maslow, and Carl Jung distinguish carefully between sexual activity and the need for intimacy. As Rollo May has said, "For human beings, the more powerful need is not for sex *per se* but for relationships, intimacy, acceptance and affirmation."

Sex is, in fact, often used as an excuse for actually avoiding intimacy. If one is afraid of the surrender required for growing intimacy, sex can be used as a cover for that fear. So at its worst, sexual exchange is judged on how well one has *avoided* getting close during the experience: "Wow, I was somewhere else that time!"

But at the same time that sex may be used as an escape from the threat of intimacy, it is also the *only* way many people know *to* be intimate. So what may happen is that the deep yearnings of two people to grow closer are frustrated by this one limited choice of love communication on which they depend for fulfillment and growth of intimacy. Every time we long for union but find that of course we are still two after orgasm, there is a sense of failure. It is not the fault of the sex act but of one's misplaced desires and expectations. Taken by itself, sex becomes an unfortunate and inappropriate catch-all for all the human love needs.

Masters and Johnson also recognized this deeper need for intimate love that goes beyond sexuality. In *The Pleasure Bond* they wrote: "Intimacy must be nourished by a mutuality between a man and a woman that may include, but must go beyond, the physical fact of intercourse. Intimacy, like any other emotion, must either grow and become deeper or it must wither and die. . . . Neither physical interchange nor physical intimacy is a sound basis for a continuing relationship."[1]

When nonsexual intimacy does grow and deepen in relationships, its growth is generally based not on wild, passionate feelings but on inner stability and security—on the deepening experience of individual personal happiness and contentment that is then shared in the relationship. Many people report that they enjoy this slowly growing kind of intimacy more than the back-and-forth instability of passion in their romantic involvements. In her study of romance, Elaine Walster concluded that at least half her subjects preferred the companion-type love of affection and deep friendship to the vagaries of "wild romance."

The intimacy of deep friendship can occur along with sexual intimacy, but sexual activity is not necessary for its growth. When this kind of intimacy does occur along with sexual expression, the experience of sexuality has been found to be very different from the overshadowing kind of sexuality that can literally take one's breath away. (During those times of "heavy breathing," we may be trying to keep our attention and feelings centered on the subtleties of sharing love, but often we're barely able to pick up the refinements in the experience because of blocked air passages caused by swollen blood vessels—a heart pumping very rapidly; we're trying to maintain heightened consciousness when everything physiological is conspiring to reduce our awareness and cut us off from the experience!)

When sex is stabilized in intimacy, another kind of experience happens. It is one of expansion, delicacy, fullness. This tender kind of sexual love is universally described as serene, nonthreatening, and comforting.

But it's not the sexual experience which brings about that serenity. One must be *already* stable and secure within oneself if one wishes to have the way opened for such intimacy to occur while maintaining sexual activity. In other words, happiness is the requirement for enjoyable sex; sex is not the basis for happiness.

CELIBACY FOR INTIMACY

Sexual love is just one kind of love. Most love relationships are celibate. Celibate love is love that could be sexual but isn't. It's true that all love has the potential to be expressed sexually, but not all love is *best* expressed sexually. Thus only a few relationships are sexual. And since celibate relationships are far more common than sexual ones, we are far more experienced in how to be celibate than in how to be sexual. Most of us have experienced how a relationship changes when it shifts from a sexual to a celibate status or vice versa. Oftentimes people may feel more comfortable and more loving in the Platonic relationships than in the more overshadowing complexities of the sexual ones. This is not because those relationships are "better": it is really because love is less likely to be restricted in its nonsexual expression than in a love relationship focused on that one overriding concern—which often occurs when sexuality dominates the relationship. Since sex tends to bring a lot of expectations with it, people tend to be more demanding in sexual affairs than in nonsexual ones. And they tend to be more disappointed in sexual relationships—due to higher expectations perhaps, but also to higher restrictions on the outcome of time spent together. Sexual relating seems to be less open-ended, less multifaceted, if only because sexual attention is trained to be drawn to the goal of activity rather than the activity itself.

Celibacy can help to break that pattern of training and limitation in love relations by removing the focus on sex in order to further explore love without the boundaries. By drawing one's love energy away from genital expression, a new range of expression is opened. Released from the one field of sexual activity, love is spontaneously transformed into a more subtle flow of energy, perhaps best thought of as a "frictionless flow"—love unimpeded by any action or by any boundary.

This flow is what celibate married couples report that they particularly enjoy: a kind of surrender in love in which feelings of tenderness grow deeper—an increasingly deeper contact. One couple described it as "a subtle but permanent orgasm, not offset by fatigue or boredom." It is love that grows automatically but does not need to be acted upon, generously available at all times. This full feeling of love is an essential part of human development and various descriptions have been put forth to explain it.

KINDS OF LOVE

The experience of love and loving changes throughout life. As one grows out of one kind of love, one becomes absorbed in the next. But one rarely learns how to integrate the easy intimacy of trust and sharing learned in nonsexual ways with the Big Adult Sexual Relationship. Often we only consider an adult relationship to be a "real" one *if* it is sexual. We forget the value of all the nonsexual relationships and the high quality of love they engender—in the quest to secure what has been designated the "best" kind of love.

Surveying the field of love from the celibate vantage point, a certain balance is gained when one realizes the extent of possibilities for real intimacy to open the heart in love—in which sexual expression is just one opportunity, and not necessarily the best one at all times.

The Primary
Love Relationship: Self-love

> The love for my own self is inseparably connected
> with the love for any other being.
> —ERICH FROMM

It is well known that the love one feels for oneself is indispensable in one's ability to love others. We learn to love ourselves through the experiences of being loved—through parents, teachers, friends, and so on. It is the way to discover one's own inner strengths and values—the secret unchanging nature of one's central being. And then we learn to love ourselves *in* others—through the opportunities they give us to love them. This basic kind of love is presexual. As psychiatrist Peter Koestenbaum describes it, "It is a transaction between one pure inward consciousness and another. The physical accoutrements are incidental, later, separate . . . [this] love is an encounter of awareness . . . [it] is thus closer to deep friendship than to sexual relations."[2]

Some evaluate self-love as the only kind of love that truly exists because it is the key ingredient in all the experiences of love one has throughout life. And the love one feels even as it extends outward is still love of oneself—you can only love anything as it expresses *you*.

So it is that self-love has many dimensions, each of which pertains to different relationships structured in different levels of consciousness or self-awareness. Many kinds of love are really simply further extensions of self-love produced by increased awareness of one's sphere of loving. Whether it is another individual, a family group, or a society to which we belong and with whom we share a common purpose—social, political, religious, scientific, artistic—whether a business, a baseball team, a nation, all the emotions and loyalties that elicit the response "LOVE" in the heart are extensions of how one feels about oneself.

Or we love ourselves in nature—seeing nature not as something *apart from* ourselves, but as a part *of* ourselves. It inspires our development; for example, we love nature as it inspires us to represent it in creations of our own—music, art, and the like—or as we create conditions to uncover its hidden mysteries in scientific laboratories or through personal exploration of its mountains and seas.

All aspects of such relationships that one has with the world are founded in the self—and certain qualities of the self grow in relation to certain experiences provided for us by nature. These are the qualities of love found in all particular relationships.

Self-Actualized Love

One of the most prominent authorities on love in recent years was the psychologist Abraham Maslow. In his studies on self-actualized people—people who were living more of their full potential in life—Maslow was able to delineate some of the ideal qualities of love.

The primary quality he found was self-sufficiency. According to his observations, self-sufficiency is the basis for love in the successful relationships of self-actualized people:

> Self-actualizing people don't *need* each other as do ordinary lovers. They can be extremely close yet go apart quite easily. . . . Throughout the most intense and ecstatic love affairs, these people remain themselves and remain ultimately masters of themselves as well, living by their own standards even though enjoying each other intensely. . . . The ego is in one sense merged with another, but yet in another sense remains separate and strong as always.

Another quality of love Maslow found to be distinguishable in self-actualized people is spontaneity: "They love because they are loving persons, in the same way that they are kind, honest, natural, i.e., because it is their nature to be so spontaneously, as a strong man is strong without willing to be, as a rose emits perfume or as a child is childish."[3]

Maslow further described love as fullness, as a quality of life which reflects fullness in waves of joy which emanate automatically from a person full of love.

Another value of love which Maslow brings to our attention is its nonpossessiveness. This quality lets love grow between people toward a kind of freedom that enables both to remain fully themselves deep within the shared experience. "In the same way," he wrote, "we can enjoy a painting without wanting to own it, a rosebush without wanting to pluck from it, a pretty baby without wanting to kidnap it . . . so also can one person admire and enjoy another in a non-doing or non-getting way."

Maslow's descriptions of qualities of love find support in the observations of many others. One well-known authority on love was the philosopher Martin Buber, who defined love as the totality of one self coming face to face with the totality of another in what he called the "I–Thou" relationship. According to Buber, the love between the two is unrestricted; it is essentially "cosmic," entirely natural, in that nature regulates it perfectly—therefore it is spontaneous, self-sufficient, always full, and certainly nonpossessive. It is likened to the air we breathe—always there generously for us to partake of it fully. And it requires another general quality of ideal love: unconditionality.

Unconditional Love:
Mother Love

A mother's love is often described as the best example of unconditional love. How the mother behaves toward her child when she herself feels happy and secure is on the basis of never-ending love. Without any struggle or effort on her part, she provides a source of constant fullness of love. She loves her child solely because it is her child. Mother's love is basically *uncontrived*, not learned or controlled. As Erich Fromm has described it, its presence "gives the loved person a sense of bliss."

It is this maternal love, the love expressed in tenderness, respect, and care that Ashley Montagu says is the "love that should and can exist between male and female" in its developed form. It is the ideal of devotional love, made all the more full when experienced by two adults who share its unconditional nurturance. Through mother's love, the child is taught to love himself or herself; through the sweetness of that love, the adult communicates his or her most intimate feelings of loving to a child and also to those precious adult friends who elicit that tender response.

Admiration, Surrender, and Devotion:
The Student/Teacher Relationship

In Eastern cultures in particular, the love for the teacher, the master, or the guide is considered perhaps the most important love relationship in life. Whether one comes upon a teacher by chance or by choice, the necessary ingredient for benefiting maximally from the relationship is said to be love. In the West too, many have experienced something of this kind of love for a grandparent or for a particular teacher in school or elsewhere who seems to have guided much of one's personal destiny and to whom one remains grateful throughout life. It is the love Beethoven is said to have felt for his teacher Carl Czerny or the love Socrates was said to have elicited from his pupils.

The specific qualities of the student love of teacher are most commonly respect, admiration, devotion, and surrender. These qualities allow the student or disciple to become wholly appreciative and therefore wholly receptive to the knowledge that the teacher offers. Based on the openness of her or his heart, the student responds with more or less openness to the teacher and, when "in love" with the teacher, is able to listen more alertly, think more attentively, and absorb the knowledge more easily.

The love represented in this relationship is the real growth of self-love which the teacher is able to facilitate by opening up a deeper part of the student's self-appreciation. The student experiences a more developed mind and a more loving heart through his devoted admiration for his "idol," thereby taking in the very qualities he loves and admires in the other. He is "pulled," as it were, "up" to his own high standards in himself through his willingness to value their expression in his teacher.

Celibate Passion: Romantic Love

Romantic love has a long history of exploration dating from the courtly love tradition of the Middle Ages. Later developments include its flowering in the Renaissance and the romantic era. Even today, it certainly has not lost much of its appeal.

In a real sense, romantic love "specializes" in celibacy. It can include sexual expression but, more typically, sexuality is the nonactive spur to the intensity of emotion which characterizes it. Since sexual relating is not the purpose or the means for establishing the relationship, the requirements of celibacy serve to free the love and the lover from what Bertrand Russell calls "all sexual alloy." Celibacy thus serves to energize the ecstasy and intense delight.

Romantic love has the distinction of being regarded as the most passionate kind of love shared between people. Its qualities are intensity, devotion, and purposeful aspiration. It is said to be based on a mysterious attraction that draws two people inevitably together: the more abstract and subtle the attraction remains, the more powerful it feels. At its best, romantic love occurs when "some enchanted evening," you see a stranger across a crowded room. But just as quickly the romance can fade when the stranger then asks you where the bathroom is.

Romantic love is really actualized in the lover's quest for the precious object of love. As the desire grows, one's heart becomes more and more full. For romantic love to achieve heights of passion, the love object may have to be difficult to attain for one reason or another—a social barrier or some other form of resistance. This is necessary because the less concrete the relationship, the better. Thus unrequited love is usually very romantic—the love object never falls from perfection because all the object of one's affection has to do is simply exist and serve as a channel for the full expression of the lover's nature, as Beatrice was for Dante.

But because it is in a sense a closed system of energy between two people meant to create a high level of concentrated feeling between the two, romantic love seems to require a way to expand in order to maintain the intensity of feeling. Otherwise, romantic love tends to "exhaust" itself, particularly as the continuation of "the feeling" is often more valued than the commitment to the person. This is perhaps why many believe that romantic love is not a good basis on which to marry, for the feeling could easily subside and become disappointment.

Platonic Love: Seeking the Ideal

Perhaps the most famous nonsexual kind of love is what we have come to call Platonic—the nonsexual intimate love between close friends. Often today Platonic love is considered less valuable than sexual love, but in Plato's day it was considered far more valuable. Sexual fulfillment, the waves of emotion so dear to the sexual lover were, for Plato, "the releasing of individual tension rather than an actual merging." But Platonic love also differs from celibate romantic love. Whereas romantic lovers are content to exchange the full measure of their feelings with each other, Platonic lovers yearn for "something bigger than both of us."

Each of us has known someone in whom we see only "the best." No matter what others may tell us or what we try to analyze intellectually, when we are with that person we see radiance and beauty. And with such a person, we feel happy and uplifted. Having experienced this feeling in one person's presence, we long to find it in another. As we search for it, what we are really seeking (says Plato) is the ideal of beauty and goodness that would make us feel most fulfilled as human beings. If we are seeking something that falls short of the ideal, we will never be satisfied. To find out what one really is looking for, Plato recommends moral teaching, a scientific education, and some form of spiritual discipline. Through self-knowledge, one learns the purpose of loving, to find the hidden values of life which bring permanent joy. This is the goal of Platonic love.

Spiritual Love

Spiritual love is really the foundation for all other kinds of love. At the same time as it is the culmination of human love (as one experiences the "divine" in others), it is also the source of all the manifestations of love. It incorporates all the qualities of love—respect, tenderness, inspiration, self-sufficiency—and all the kinds of love relationships within its sphere and gives them the maximum chance for development. It is spiritual love which has been found to be the most unbounded, the most freeing, the most elevating, and the most developed kind of love humanly possible.

Spiritual love has been recognized throughout the ages as the ideal vehicle for seeking perfection in life. It has been declared the means by which we transcend the limits of "ordinary" love to discover a deeper aspect of the heart's possibilities on another plane.

It is often understood in terms of its expression of divinity. And for some, the knowledge and experience of the divine is the only reason for human love to exist—in its representation of the divine on earth. As writer C. S. Lewis contends, "Human loves deserved to be called loves at all just in so far as they resembled the love which is God."

This kind of spiritualized love was first described in ancient Greece and was called *agape*—the opposite of *eros*—meaning "nonerotic." It was really a description of the religious love relationship: the devotion of the worshiper for the worshiped. Agape love is seen as a love that liberates, that does not possess, as a source of perfection and spiritual energy.

But spiritual love does not have to take on the value of the divine and the "godly." In his studies on love, Maslow found it unnecessary to distinguish between the spirituality of godly love and the spirituality of human love. He pointed out that the attempt to differentiate the two was usually based on the misunderstanding that pure admiration and "objective" devotional love could be only superhuman qualities, not normal human ones, a point his research contradicted.

Spiritual love might also be characterized as the most refined form of sexual love—a form considered in other eras to be most satisfying. Spiritual love relationships are difficult for us to consider today, but in other eras the experience of this spiritual love between man and woman, contends Richardson, "was so startling and so satisfying that for a thousand years the practice of perpetual virginity was chosen as the way to love more fully. . . ."[4]

As celibacy is one way of expressing sexual love in its most universal, most spiritualized state, it is often a testimony to a spiritual commitment. In one sense, spiritual love forces us to surrender all weaknesses and limitations in the personality by creating a condition for bringing out "the best" in us. And as sexuality becomes a restriction in the expression of one's true self, it too must be surrendered to a higher form of expression. It is a vital and necessary part of self-development. To accept one's spiritual needs and desires is as necessary for one's personal growth as the acceptance of one's sexuality. Both are part of developing the ability to love and the capacity for intimacy.

The Goal of Love: Union

> And neither the angels in Heaven above
> Nor the drones down under the sea
> Can ever dissever my soul from the soul
> Of the beautiful Annabel Lee.
> —EDGAR ALLEN POE

The goal of all love is said to be growth to the point of full merging of the "souls" or full development of consciousness to experience union—and to live in unity with all aspects of nature, whether one other human being or all things in the universe.

Until this awareness of union is appreciated, a person may have tried for union only through sexual union. But as one matures, a different view of personal union may start to develop—a union based on spiritual love.

The concept of union or merging with the divine is found in most religions. God is thought to be everywhere and in everything, so it is possible to merge with the divine always, as long as one has first established oneself as a separate expression of divinity. Once one's divine self is realized, God is indeed seen everywhere and the individual self, surrendering, is "dissolved like a lump of salt in the ocean" but, at the same time, takes on the status of the ocean. And in all spiritual experiences, once one has recognized divinity, it is inevitable that one will want to know more of it. This desire is what propels the continuing growth of love; it is the impetus to merge with someone you love or even the whole universe on a much deeper basis than a physical connection. This feeling, writes Elizabeth Haich, "has nothing to do with sexual desire, nothing whatsoever to do with the body, for we certainly have no sensual-sexual desire towards the whole wide world, and yet the feeling is there: a purely spiritual feeling, a purely spiritual state."[5]

This growth of love is understandably a real substitute for and even an improvement over sex. And it gives us an insight into why some people are willing and able to love and live celibately.

In the following two chapters, celibacy for men and for women is explored in light of particular physical, psychological, and social insights and information specific to each sex.

Each chapter also includes interviews with men and women who have experienced being celibate and who share their reactions to that experience. For the most part they are successful, positive, strong people with a goal of personal fulfillment in life. They all seemed quite happy and were remarkably "healthy-looking." They all had had sexual experience—some more and some less extensive than average. None seemed to really dislike sex; rather, the emphasis was on enjoying other things more. They considered their celibacy a natural part of their own personal growth, something inevitable, based on a combination of internal and external factors, but definitely something of their own choosing. Most were involved in some kind of program of self-development, although no program had directed them to become celibate. That seemed to be a decision arising out of their own life experiences. In general, they were into healthy living: good food, exercise, no drugs, and so on.

On the whole, they seemed to be quite private about celibacy. They were strongly committed to being celibate, if only temporarily, but each concurred that he or she would not tell many others about it. Some were particularly careful that their families did not know, because they felt the families would have difficulty understanding. Each felt celibacy offered valuable opportunities for growth in their relationships and within themselves but were not interested in promoting it as a "cause." They considered themselves private explorers, not social innovators.

However, those who knew other celibate people felt that this was an important factor in their continuing commitment. They liked the idea of being able to talk about celibacy in a supportive environment with friends who were also experimenting in this way. None thought that they would necessarily be celibate forever; the overall approach seemed to be to maintain it as long as it provided positive benefits in their lives.

The
Celibate Man

MEN REACT
TO THE SEXUAL REVOLUTION

4 In a word: "Help!

Most men have been more-than-willing participants in the sexual revolution, but some have
been its victims as well. Certainly, men now have a much
greater opportunity to accomplish the Great American Goal
of constant sexuality and are well supplied with the
necessary media materials on almost every downtown
corner and in almost every daily environment from office to
home. And finding an agreeable partner is now quite possible on a first date.

Of course, there are new responsibilities that come
with these new opportunities. The major one is the issue of
women's newly embraced sexual lives. Due to the widespread research and clearly revised resulting information
on women's sexuality that has substantially formed the
sexual revolution, men today feel they must perform not
only in keeping with the greater availability of sexual encounters but also to meet the needs of knowledgeable
women.

And so, for many men, sexual performance has become a major challenge. One feature of this challenge is

to prolong intercourse. In a study for *Playboy* magazine, Morton Hunt found that the length of duration of male intercourse has changed from the reported two minutes in Kinsey's survey in the early 1950s to an average of ten minutes in the late 1970s: "It would appear that nowadays the sexually liberated, thoroughly motivated young man can hold himself back, and possesses both the physical and psychic energy to outlast the older man." But not all can.

The "New Impotence"
There is little doubt that most men today are intent upon being not just lovers, but good lovers. But sadly, some men and some women mistake that for being good performers. And so, Hunt discovered, the current sexual standards have given rise (or perhaps given fall) to an emerging problem of impotence among younger men. He reports that a growing number of young husbands fail to have orgasms over half the time when they make love—something not found in Kinsey's day. Hunt attributes this "new impotence" to the assertiveness of women, which he sees as a result of the impact of the women's liberation movement.

Whether or not this is a correct understanding, it is true that sexual activity has become more problematic for a number of men. Not only must they allay their own fears and anxieties about sex, but now they must respond according to the needs and anxieties of women whose emerging sexual freedom is no less fraught with complications. And men can't even fake it when they have to. So, as a result, some men are becoming more anxious about performance, some even impotent, and, in general, sex may be presenting more problems than before the revolution.

Not only do men have to deal with the perceived demands stemming from the new sexuality, they also must deal with overcoming the limitations of the lifelong societal lessons on how to be a successful man. The prevailing male lesson is that masculinity is sexual, and performance and equipment count for almost the whole ballgame. A "real" man performs correctly if: (1) He has a sexual desire, (2) he has an erection, and (3) he has an orgasm. Feelings of love and tenderness are optional but should not distract from the pleasures of genital feelings and the freedom to gratify the desire immediately and easily.

When we say a man is soft, we usually mean that he's not altogether there. He can easily be fooled, as in "he's a soft touch" or he's mentally ill as in "he's soft in the head." In general, in our culture to be soft is to be a failure if you are a man. Not just sexually but in every way. All the qualities associated with masculine sexuality have come to be equated with masculinity in general. A *man*, "The Man of La Macho," is hard, tough as nails. Just as it's good to be hard when you're sexually aroused, it's good to be hard when your emotions, intimate feelings, and desires are on the line. This distortion of male development has presented men in this society with a major dilemma. By concentrating his emotional capabilities on a sexual focus, a man must restrict his full range of expression to those qualities considered right for sexual activity specifically (i.e., hardness, performance) and even limited there.

By restricting masculinity and male image to the sexual arena, self-image becomes entirely sexualized. In this way, fears and anxieties coming from other aspects of male growth settle here. Sex becomes almost the only acceptable measure of male success and, consequently, of alleviating other, nonsexual tensions.

Male Intimacy

If sexual activity is the modus operandi of being male, then men must be taught to avoid other less "manly" forms of self-expression. And indeed they are—from infancy on. As Ashley Montagu points out in his writings on love and intimacy, girl babies receive more affection through touch than boys. He sees this tactile deprivation reflected later in the typical roughness of the male during genital lovemaking.

As the sexual becomes the only acceptable channel for

male intimacy to express itself, deeper needs for intimacy become repressed or unexpressed. Unable to express himself in the deeper levels of intimate loving, a man may become fearful of these deeper levels and intimacy-related anxieties develop which he feels he must avoid at all costs. Quite simply, sex becomes a way for the man to avoid intimacy and expression of a more profound part of himself. And thus sex takes on a greater additional burden, that of relieving anxiety in men who have been taught that sexual tension means a possible confrontation with their deeper needs.

For many men, therefore, sex has a great big job to do quite apart from fulfilling sexual desires. It has to avoid intimacy, relieve anxiety, cover fears, and express a man's full development as a masculine person. It is little wonder that most men have some uneasiness regarding their sexual abilities.

Male Fantasy

It is often assumed that women are the romanticizers and fantasizers, the dreamers and emotional pushovers. However, in her study of romantic love, Dr. Elaine Walster found that men are really more romantic than women. Contrary to widespread belief, she noted that it is men who fall in love more quickly and women who are more careful and practical when it comes to a romantic commitment. Although women are most involved and consumed at the height of a passionate affair, men tend to be more overshadowed and tend to cling to a waning romance with greater desperation.

Furthermore, male sexuality has been commonly understood to be oriented to physical need, whereas female sexuality has been thought to be more emotionally based, relying on fantasy for initiating desire. In actuality, men have been found to have far more sexual fantasies and a far greater emotional commitment to sex than women—most likely due to cultural bias favoring sex for men.

And if they can't live out sex in reality, many men lead full and complex sex lives on the level of fantasy. Women tend to think less about sex when they are not involved in a sexual relationship, whereas men tend to continue to think about it. It has been reported that many men really want to escape from the bonds of fantasy living; some even say they have sex simply in order to be free from sexualizing for a time afterward. It isn't sexual activity per se that they want to be free of; it's the time they waste thinking about sex—a kind of never-ending mental loop continually rewound through lifelong habits and cultural reinforcement.

Looking more deeply at the ability of men to fantasize sex, one finds an important understanding about male sexuality that may have been overlooked: the interior ability of men to completely govern their own sexuality—sexuality that has often been viewed as quite automatic and uncontrollable. In fact, it has been found that some men, with proper training, can fantasize physical orgasms (and can achieve multiple orgasms in this way). In his research on spinal-cord–injured individuals, Dr. Theodore Cole found a number of cord-injured men who could achieve each mental state of the progression to orgasm and experience the sensation of its physical counterpart from excitation through ejaculation.

In interviewing one such man for this book—a twenty-seven-year-old video engineer named Richard—the author learned that he was able to transfer his sensual/sexual energy from the lower disabled part of his body to the upper part, particularly his chest area. What was significant was that he was also able to realize an ability to shift this energy anywhere in his body, even entirely to his mind. Here are some of his comments,

> I have ways of rechanneling my genital sexual energy, but I have a lot to learn sexually about myself even after two years of being disabled. I think I am more aware of women on a deeper level since my response is more a psychological re-

lease. I maintain a very intense level of feeling, and I have this driving energy which seems to have a lot of power. Instead of diminishing it through genital release like I used to, it seems to get greater. Recently, I had my first orgasm learned in this way. I concentrated my energy on my chest, but I know I could train any part of my body to respond sexually. It feels as though I am expanding to experience the full force of the energy. I watch it happen while I experience it and forget that there is an act or an experience. I seem to go beyond that spectrum. I'm not bowled over by a physical release, but I do experience a profound warmth and lightness spreading throughout my body.

I feel I have unlimited energy. A lot of my physical energy goes into sports, i.e., wheelchair basketball. I had never really used my body before the accident, and now I really enjoy using it.

I also find that my energy goes into my mental and creative work. I can spend six or seven hours at a time focusing on what I am doing without getting spaced out. I also notice that more and more I can intuitively know things I want to know—I've always had some ability like this, but now I use it much more.

I also think that I have a lot of personal attraction for others. People seem to be drawn to me even when I'm just sitting quietly. I don't think it's because I'm in a wheelchair—more because I feel very stable; my energy feels very self-contained, and I must radiate some of that.

This energy-transfer ability is an indication that men have a far greater capacity for experiencing their sexual energy in other than genital ways than they have been taught to imagine. In the East, for example, masculinity and virility are understood to be the result of rechanneling sexual energy into higher pursuits. Conservation of this energy and the corresponding physical retention of the seminal fluid are considered imperative in a man's growth toward spiritual fulfillment and enlightenment.

Throughout Western history, a more narrow view of man's physical debilitation resulting from sexual excess is a common theme. In the twelfth century, the Jewish philosopher and physician Moses Maimonides warned: "Effusion of semen represents the strength of the body and its life and the light of the eyes. Whenever it is emitted to excess, the body becomes consumed, its strength terminates, and its life perishes." He goes on to say that excessive sex can cause premature lapses in memory, mental debility, faulty digestion, and defective vision.

Similarly, in the first decades of this century in America, the "alarming" results of male sexual excess were presented by a number of physicians, often in connection with a holistic approach to health, including the need for nutritional programs such as vegetarianism, some form of exercise, and an appeal to renounce liquor and smoking as well as sex.

One such physician, Dr. Arthur Gould, wrote a lengthy treatise on the ill effects of too much sex and despaired: "Modern man cannot be convinced that his perpetual appetite for indulgence is not perfectly natural, even praiseworthy." And only fifty years ago, another writer gloomily detailed: "The too great loss of the seminal fluid soon produces upon men effects very analogous with those of castration, such as weakness, dejection of mind, debility, and pusillanimity, together with all that mental timidity which exaggerates the least dangers and succumbs under the most trivial apprehensions."[1]

In other words, too much sex makes Jack not simply a dull boy but a paranoid schizophrenic. But if a man is celibate, observed Dr. Gould, the "excessive secretions of the vital fluids decrease and are absorbed into the ductless glands," and the energy is maintained—a process which he said was similar to the experience of early youth prior to sexual activity.

This line of thought sounds pretty arcane to us now, but the question is whether the current emphasis on "use it or lose it" is any less naïve. Just because modern researchers have not found any major debilitating effects of sexual activity in the average man does not mean that some effects do not exist in some men. As a matter of fact, very little is known about the physical effects of sexuality in the individual male.

In general, sexual arousal and activity leading to orgasm produce rapid physiological changes. Heart rate doubles, breath rate triples, blood pressure rises considerably, to name a few. Seminal fluid has been found to contain biologically significant nutrients. A continuous flow of sperm is produced as the blood flows through the testes (where a temperature four degrees cooler than the rest of the body is maintained). During an average ejaculation, one-half billion sperm are released from the body. After intercourse, it takes a single sperm about thirty minutes to reach the womb.

It has been found that the amount of seminal fluid is related to the subjective quality of the orgasm. Kinsey's research demonstrated that if a man is low on seminal fluid, the orgasm will not feel as enjoyable. He also found that preadolescent boys have the ability to have multiple orgasms, an ability they tend to lose "at the age when the male climax starts to be accompanied by the ejaculation of semen." So there is a relationship at least between the amount saved and the amount spent in regard to the quality of the sexual experience.

Now it may be true that a lot of sex "can't hurt," but it is also true that many men do feel some weakening effects following ejaculation, often even for a day or two afterward. Each man's individual physiology must be taken into account. The point is that to dismiss a man's postsexual fatigue as a mental rather than physical problem is to neglect all the possible physiological realities of any particular body. It's really no different to declare that all men feel good after sex than to say that all men become weakened and paranoid afterward.

A related aspect of male sexual functioning is the effect of celibacy.

THE REALITIES OF CELIBACY:
CAN MEN DO WITHOUT SEX?

Seminal fluid is produced continuously in a man's body; at times its abundance may cause a physical tension. It is this physical tension which has brought about the misunderstanding that men "need" sex and cannot be celibate.

In reality, in studying the effects of the retention of seminal fluid, Kinsey reported that in comparing celibate men with sexually active men, he did *not* find more nocturnal emissions or any other spontaneous indicators of the male need for physical relief through ejaculation. Kinsey further observed that there is no physiological reason for a man to have a real physical discomfort from lack of sexual release: "There is a popular opinion that the testes are the sources of the semen which the male ejaculates. The testes are supposed to become swollen with accumulated secretions between the times of sexual activity, and periodic ejaculation is supposed to be necessary in order to relieve these pressures. . . . Most of these opinions are, however, quite unfounded."[2]

Kinsey goes on to say that if there is discomfort as the result of unrelieved erotic arousal, it is located in the surrounding musculature and not in the testes and/or sexual organs themselves. And obviously, if sexual arousal does not occur regularly, there can be no reason for any physical difficulties.

What Kinsey did find was that men in situations requiring celibacy are much more comfortable than expected. For one thing, without external sexual stimuli, male sexual desire tends to diminish. Kinsey's research of sex in prison life in the 1940s led to his observation that when men are in nonerotic situations or environments (for example, short-term prison), they adjust to celibacy even for a year at a time. "Most of them live comfortably enough apparently because there is little erotic arousal which needs to be relieved by orgasm."

For another thing, as time goes on, the less sex men engage in, the less they desire it. The longer a man is celibate, the easier it becomes for him to be celibate. In his research on male sexuality, Dr. Bernard Zilbergeld found that men who are celibate are not plagued by "consuming sexual appetites." Shere Hite reached similar conclusions—that men don't really need sex as often as they think they do.

In addition, men may think they need sex because even if they were physically comfortable, their fantasies would overwhelm them. In this regard, some men interviewed for a *New York Times* article on celibacy expressed interest in celibacy but were afraid to try it for fear of having to live with *more* sexual fantasies.

As more research on male sexuality and celibacy is carried out, more detailed documentation of the effects of both on a man's health and activities will enable us to have a more complete picture. What has been most valued—the male orgasm—may turn out to deserve less value. But as are now, orgasm is *the* predominant goal of male sexuality.

Male Orgasm

If the importance of female orgasm has been under-emphasized, to say the very least, the importance of male orgasm has been greatly exaggerated.
—SHERE HITE

According to the Kinsey research, unmarried males between the ages of sixteen and twenty years ejaculate an average of over three times a week or about once every two days. He found daily orgasm to be "well within the capacity of the young male." Married men had the highest number of orgasms per week (about five) but after age thirty, two times a week was the average. For men over seventy, it was found to be about once every two weeks. Other studies have demonstrated that, in general, male sexuality and potency continue even beyond the seventies as long as the brain chemistry and chemical circuits to other parts of the body still respond to sexual arousal.

So it is apparent that if you are a male, having orgasms is not too big a deal. It is likely that you have the capability to have them all your life if you want. Indeed, even the "schlepps" have them. In his film *Manhattan,* the ever-neurotic Woody Allen character, responding to a woman's concern that after she finally had her first orgasm her doctor informed her that it was the wrong kind, says, "Mine are always the right kind. Even my worst one was right on the money!"

Yet even though men have them easily enough, orgasms have somehow become a tremendous sexual goal for men. In our culture, for a man to have an erection and lose it through an orgasm is considered to be, by and large, the definition of male sexuality and, consequently, male virility and masculinity. This orgasm focus continues throughout a man's life, even when it is not socially necessary for procreation or for good sex.

The Older Man
As a man gets older, the orgasm mode of sexual functioning continues to be the "correct" expression of a man's vitality and ability to love. Even though older men have less physical desire to have an orgasm, the psychological dependence that has been created throughout a lifetime may never diminish. Thus a great fear of adult males in our society is of the "male menopause"—a time when procreative genital function has changed to a more diffuse sexuality—and many men despair that they will become less manly, less sexual, and therefore, less alive.

Joseph Wade, in his studies of sex and celibacy in church life, distinguished between a physical desire for sexual expression which he, like Kinsey, observed to diminish after age thirty and a psychological "need" for sex based on social training, which may never diminish.

Thus, as men get older, many find that their sexual needs continue, although the need is generally psychological rather than somatic.

For an older man, celibacy may seem to be more a reluctant resignation than a real choice. It is definitely considered a choice for a younger man who is thought to be functioning at full sexual steam and therefore has something to be celibate about. But an older man may see celibacy as a final defeat in his battle to uphold waning virility. This is a very unfortunate distortion. For once masculinity and virility are seen for what they really are, sexuality becomes a *restriction* on their development.

The value of age—with its accompanying realization of who one is and what one wants, of wisdom, of the release from the social straits of "what others think of me," of the profound vision of seeing what one's real commitments in life are: these are the glory of the older man. Certainly men can feel sexy and have orgasms even in their eighties, but to hold on to that limited view of self-worth when one has finally reached a pinnacle of fullness in life—this can really diminish a man's strength and status in the world.

Few things are as embarrassing as one age trying to be another. Just as we feel uncomfortable around somber, adultlike children "wise beyond their years," we naturally feel uncomfortable around men or women trying to be adolescents—not only for the futility of their efforts, but also for the waste of their precious adulthood in favor of a less developed status.

A virile man is one who is what he is—fully established in his own being—not one who tries to be what he was at a younger age thereby denying his present self.

A broader vision of manliness that presents men with a more complete picture of the nature of virility, of strength, of masculine prowess is needed. In this regard, it is useful to look at some other views of male sexuality and celibacy.

The Macho Celibate: The Masculine
Virtue of Sexual Abstinence

In our culture, male celibacy has been generally associated with strict religious vocation or with extenuating social situations such as wartime or the death of a spouse. Not until recently has any thought been given to *choosing not* to express one's maleness through sexuality. But in most other times and cultures, the expression of male sexuality has not been the exclusive basis for proving oneself to be a man: in other words, what has been considered truly masculine, strong, and virile has not been ordinarily confined to sexual activity.

Although there has been a widespread tendency for cultures to equate male sexuality with power, in most societies such power has been equated not with the participation in sexual activity but with the *withholding* of sexuality. "Celibate prowess," not sexual prowess, has been most often regarded as the real proving ground for the challenge of masculine strength.

Such an attitude may emerge following prior excessive sexual activity. As Bertrand Russell wrote in *Marriage and Morals,* "Men who are not restrained by a fairly rigid ethic are apt to indulge to excess: This produces in the end a feeling of weariness . . . which leads naturally to ascetic convictions." Obviously, the pendulum has swung back many times before: There have been many "lusty" societies in the history of the world for which celibacy must have provided a welcome relief. For example, in ancient Rome despite its dissolute reputation, the effort of continence was greatly admired and thought to represent a superior nature and a character verging on the divine.

Courtly Love:
The Male Celibate Tradition

Perhaps the most notable period of male secular celibacy occurred during the Middle Ages when the tradition of courtly love was at its height and when masculine sexuality was successfully transformed into devotional service and spiritual love. It was the duty of the knight to devote himself unselfishly to the noble lady. The knight would thus offer his full strength to his lady for whom he fought in battle and for whom he contained his sexuality. This ritual of the Middle Ages was called *māze*—the power of devotional love created by the withholding of sexual activity.

In his description of the courtly love tradition, which later came to be called the tradition of romantic love, Dr. Hugo Beigel writes: "In spite of the surface appearance of its aesthetic formulation, it sprang from vital needs, from a deeply-felt desire for the ennoblement of human relations. . . . It made māze (or moderation) a masculine virtue."[3]

The actual arrangements between the knights and their ladies occurred only *outside* marriage: "Being the spiritualization and the sublimation of carnal desire, such love was deemed to be impossible between husband and wife." This was due to the Christian idea that sex was wholly incompatible with spirituality; in this light a sexual marriage had no place for spiritual growth. These spiritually elevating relations could, therefore, only be established between the knight and the lady. This arrangement for a spiritual relationship was called *minne* and was based on absolute chastity. Within the tradition, the woman was idealized and elevated. Respect for her high position induced devotion, tenderness and restraint in the male worshiper. For the woman, loyalty to her husband was separate from her loyalty to her gallant. Of course, being married, she herself was not able to be celibate; she was merely an object of love through which the knight could achieve his own uplift.

In such a state, the knight's love was said to flower and, indeed, become a spiritual experience rising on increasingly higher planes of devotional feeling. Safely kept from sexual expression, so-called "love tests" were undertaken by the lovers.

The test of *drutz* was considered the "Black Belt" of courtly love—the highest state of the art. The knight or gallant was allowed into the lady's bedchamber, permitted to undress her completely, to put her to bed, and even to kiss her and sleep with her in a nonsexual embrace.

This spiritual love actually opened the way for the later tradition of romantic love, which still later became sexualized. But advocates of the courtly love or romantic tradition devoid of sexual activity consider it one of the high points in the history of love of men for women.

THE TREND TO CELIBACY: WHY MEN DO WITHOUT SEX

In the early 1950s, in his research on celibacy, Albert C. Kinsey found that in men under the age of thirty, abstinence was common for a few days or a week at a time, but only 11 percent reported being abstinent for longer than two weeks at a time and only 3 percent were abstinent for ten weeks or longer. Kinsey further observes in his report that most men he interviewed would have been ashamed to report any lack of sexual activity because the social pressure to be sexually active was too great. So he was not convinced of the accuracy of those figures.

In their book *The Virile Man,* Sheldon Fellman and Paul Neimark see celibacy as a very positive alternative for some men. Dr. Fellman, a urologist, has found about one in every thirty or forty men to be "unconcerned with sex"; often he is "a man who wants to devote all his energies to his work."

Isaac Newton, Immanuel Kant, William Pitt, Martin Luther, Beethoven, Sigmund Freud, Anthelme Brillat-Savarin, George Bernard Shaw, Henry David Thoreau, and Alfred Hitchcock are some well-known men who practiced celibacy for all or part of their lives. There have no doubt been many successful secular celibates who did not necessarily give up social life or even marriage in order to remain nonsexual. In all likelihood, male celibacy has become more acceptable as more men find it useful in their lives. Its usefulness ranges from a cure for impotence to a commitment of all sexual energy for spiritual life.

Celibacy has been a recognized cure for impotence for centuries. In his writings on male sexuality, Maimonides prescribed celibacy as the necessary antidote to impotence resulting from a variety of causes including sexual fatigue. And today, a large number of doctors and therapists are recommending celibacy for men to help alleviate the stress associated with sex and the pressure to perform in specified ways. Celibacy is said to "center" the impotent man by allowing him to stay within himself, to rest, to regroup his resources and to rechannel his blocked energy. And, let's face it, it's a lot more interesting to be celibate than impotent.

There may be a tendency to want to relate the "new impotence" with the "new celibacy," but they are totally different—in fact, celibacy is the opposite of impotence. An impotent man wants to have sex but cannot perform, whereas a celibate man can perform but does not want to have sex. Indeed, celibacy can be considered "the source of the very highest potency." Haich describes the enlightened celibates whose energies have been directed to other than sexual goals. The body, she says, at these higher energy levels, "lives with much greater intensity and has much greater potency than the body of a man who is still in the grip of sexuality and expends life-giving energy." Furthermore, she emphasizes that "these enlightened men did not become impotent, no matter how often ignorant people may claim the contrary."

Celibacy and Relationships
Eugene Bianchi, a Jesuit who was celibate for twenty years prior to marriage, studied celibacy within the church and observed a distinction between physical celibacy and what he calls psychic celibacy. He says that the psychic celibate

keeps women at arm's length, not only physically but mentally and emotionally as well. Women are seen primarily as embodiments of "the temptress"; in order to maintain psychic celibacy, women are excluded on *all* levels of relating.

It's true that quite a few men see women as exclusively sexual—and are thus unable to separate their emotional relationships with women from the sexual components. And if they become celibate, they think that they must keep entirely separate from women. One scientist interviewed by *The New York Times* reported that after a year of being celibate, what he missed most was "not sex but the closeness you feel in a primary relationship." It is unfortunate that closeness and sexuality were so intricately bound that he did not have the opportunity to experience a close relationship while celibate.

The truth of the matter is that celibacy can be a great help to men by allowing them to experience growth in relationships without the set patterns imposed by sexual habits and expectations.

And, as a bonus, celibate men who are open to relating to women find that women are very attracted to them. There seems to be a kind of personal strength and charisma that celibate men manifest. A celibate man who has freely chosen to be celibate and is comfortable with it offers other people the chance to see themselves reflected in his eyes and heart in other than sexual ways. It's a great gift to "see" and "be seen" without the imposition of the dominating sexual viewpoint.

Celibacy can help a man explore new modes of personal communication and intimate relating with others. It can enable a man to pursue a variety of goals such as deepening his commitment to achievement in work or spending more time with his children or other perhaps more spiritual goals. Celibacy can provide a way for a man to open his heart to his lovers, friends, and family; to break boundaries in his own emotional life; to get more deeply involved with his own nonsexual priorities. It can help a man see his life more clearly, take control of his activities, learn to choose what he wants and who he wants it with. It can help him take charge of his mind and his body, and it can enable him to come to grips with his masculinity by allowing him to separate his virility from his sexuality.

In all, celibacy can both strengthen a man and soften him; it can allow him to experience the unboundedness of his settled being, to experience the expansion of his heart and mind into other areas of relating and accomplishing. He can expand his life without losing his focus on personal growth at the expense of a habit he no longer wants to be bound by. Celibacy can free him to look at his own sexual life, to put in perspective what place he wants sex to have in his daily experience and to find what other possibilities are available to him.

FIVE CELIBATE MEN

Carl: age twenty-eight, auto salesman

"I have been celibate for two years, since my divorce. I was married for three and a half years and when the marriage was over, I went through a heavy "proving" time, making sure I was still desirable and sexy to women. I actually looked up my old high school flames and had several affairs. I have always been a real "mover" sexually—always looking for the next sexual experience before I was even finished with the current one.

I do remember just when I decided to be celibate. I was driving late one night, and I stopped at a traffic light. My window was rolled down, and this girl at the corner came up and asked me if I wanted a date. It turned me on, and we ended up in bed and I got VD. I felt really gross and nasty—had some bummer moments at the doctor's office— "Oh, you're the one with the gonorrhea," etc. I decided that it was really ridiculous to be so dominated by sex that I really ended up feeling miserable. Somehow this experience was a sign that I'd better take a little responsibility for myself and what I was doing. So I decided intellectually to be celibate.

I say intellectually because I am still very sexual. But, lo and behold, I found that I could contain my sexual impulses pretty easily and be free of that constant push to get into bed with someone. I found that the desire would come, but if I didn't act on it, it wouldn't be as strong. Every time I was horny and didn't "do it," either find a woman to sleep with or masturbate, I wouldn't be as horny the next time the desire came up. I did stop masturbating almost entirely and feel good about it.

When I am happy, it's very easy to be celibate. When I'm unhappy, it's more difficult, and I start to get sexually turned on. I know that I have pretty much used sex as a way to relieve frustration in other areas of my life, even when I was married. I think that being celibate has given me a great deal more stability in my life and allowed me to have much better relationships with women. You'd be surprised how many women are turned on by a celibate man. It gives them a chance to be themselves without sex and still get loved.

I don't know how much longer I'll be celibate. I basically take it on a day-to-day basis. I don't want to feel like I'm holding back some part of me, but I do think by consciously avoiding sex, I've opened up a whole new field for my personality to express itself. And I do feel a lot better about myself.

What about "blue balls"? Am I uncomfortable physically, not being sexually active? No, not all all. If I don't put myself in a tempting situation, I don't get turned on and avoid the frustration. The whole feeling is very liberating for a man."

Brent, age twenty-two, student

"I've never been in love the way I fantasize love. I spent about six years trying to live out my fantasies, and it didn't really work. I've thought about sex since I was very young.

I think I've been more sexually consumed in fantasy than most.

The big thing in college of course has been "progressive" sex—how far you can go and how soon—i.e., "scoring." Consequently, most of my sexual experience has been "one-nighters." Until I was twenty, I was part of the "if-it-feels-good, do-it" school. I probably slept with about forty different women. Usually, I separated my women "friends" from my sexual companions. Like I'd say, "She means more to me as a friend." I guess I must have thought it was more of a compliment to a girl not to have sex with her.

When I was twenty, I met a woman with whom I had a long-term affair—a year and a half—based pretty much on sex. I wasn't in love with her, but I was comfortable with her. There wasn't a lot of guilt. It was a real time of sexual exploration but also a realization that I wanted more than sex from a relationship. We were very different: sex is what kept us together, but, basically, I was bored. Eventually, sex wasn't enough. After we broke up, I almost started being promiscuous again, but somehow it didn't have the same pull as before. It seems that I had to choose between promiscuity and celibacy. So I've been celibate for about a year.

There's a part of me that would hop into anyone's bed, and there's a stronger part of me that wants to find someone who turns me on more than sexually. It's easy to turn me on sexually. I feel good about anyone who wants my body. I know, however, that I want to take my time and really find what I want and get to know someone. It's hard to put out energy and not have it come back.

I've been getting closer to my male friends as the result of this period of celibacy. It seems that because I'm not being sexual, I'm not as threatened getting close to men. At the same time, I think I'm getting closer to women. I live with a woman who has a child and even though it's nonsexual, I really enjoy the warmth of a kind of family life with her.

I used to get sex confused with other things. I was real tied into how others see me. My worth was verified by someone wanting to have sex with me, so not having sex made me feel deprived. Now, sex for me has got to be connected with another person, with emotions; it can't just be sex for sex's sake. My standards for what I want have gotten higher, I think. I'm more concerned with the quality of how I feel about the person.

Since I've been celibate, sex is less on my mind than it used to be. This surprised me because I thought I'd think more about it. I actually have less sexual fantasies than before. It was too frustrating and as I started getting other strokes in other areas, the fantasies went away. I think I became more involved in other parts of my life. Masturbation too has decreased from once a day to less than once a week. It seems that it's easier for me to forego sex now than when I first stopped having it.

I know I haven't given up sex at all. I'm just looking for the right person to share it with. I'm interested in getting married and having a family, and I guess that, strange as it may seem, this time of celibacy is preparing me for that kind of commitment. Otherwise, I'd still be running around with as many women as I could find to get it on with. And I'd still be feeling worthless and frustrated. This way, I feel like even though I'd rather be involved with someone than not, it's in my own interests to be celibate until I find what I am looking for, and not waste my time, energy, and thoughts on unrewarding people and experiences."

John: age twenty-seven, architect

"I've been celibate for about a year and have been openly gay for over seven years. Before that I had some not-too-successful experiences with women. I lived with one man for two and one-half years and have definitely had my share of sexual experiences with other men.

When I decided to be celibate, it was an impulsive kind of thing—as if to say "Stop all this nonsense." I had begun to feel really trapped by what I consider pretty typical gay male behavior. Maybe it's also typical of other people, I don't know. Basically, it seemed that the possibilities of relating to another man who is also gay begin with sex and end when sex ends. I know this isn't just true for me. Of course, I do know some gay couples for whom sex has become just one part of the relationship, and I even know a completely celibate gay couple, but in my experience, most gays are largely dominated by sexual relating at the expense of other kinds.

Once you've experienced the exhilaration and freedom of expressing love for your own sex, you realize how great a distance is yet to go. Many gays, once they've "come out," tend to stop relating beyond sex. In a way, it was a lot more interesting to meet other men before it was so acceptable to be gay. Mainly because there was no guarantee that sex was going to be part of the experience, and you would spend a lot of time getting to know each other before "the big revelation." I think gay life is so sexual because that's the part of the personality which is identified. It seems really unfair to me. I like sex, don't get me wrong, but I really get off on the emotional involvement with men.

There is this article—an interview with Quentin Crisp—the man on whom the TV play *The Naked Civil Servant* was based. I saved it and would like to have some of it quoted as part of the interview because I agree with what he says, and I think he says it very well, if a little intensely.

> As soon as you know a person, sex is over. All married couples find this. You may seek sex elsewhere, but your relationship is no longer supported by its sexuality. . . . With homosexuals, it's more extreme. They try to find situations in which the person with whom they are having some kind of sexual relationship cannot have time to utter a word for fear they would reveal something about themselves and become a person.
> If you are happy, you don't pursue sex in this frantic way that homosexuals do. Whether you are sexually happy is not the point. If you're happy, if you have a nice life, if you do a

job that other people tell you you do well, then you live contentedly. Sex is an illness, a fever. And this perpetual search for pleasure is always undertaken by people who have no happiness.[4]

Since I've been celibate, some good things have been growing in me. For one thing, I've stopped relating to people in a predominantly sexual way—I've stopped relating to men as sexual objects and women as sexual threats. I've also more or less forced others to see *me* in other ways, too. Which has been very important to me.

I like relating to women as a celibate man. It takes a lot of the tension away because it takes the sexual "challenge" of homosexuality away. Women I know were often out to be the one who reforms me. Now it's a more natural kind of relating. They see me now not as a disappointment but as a man with a lot to offer them that other men don't give them. And with straight men too I'm more comfortable. If they're threatened by me, I know it's their trip because I know I'm not doing any challenging.

So I feel much more open in all my relationships. I feel like I've grown a lot emotionally, become stronger, more independent. My work has really progressed, and I've had much more opportunity to get into it in a profound way. I don't know if that has to do with being celibate, but I have noticed that my attention is much more solid and focused, and I feel more calm inside. I don't know how long I'll remain celibate, but it's certainly been good for me. Some friends were very skeptical about my motivations at first— they thought it was sort of phony, but they've definitely changed their opinion since they've seen me change and now they too seem interested in being less involved in sex and more involved in living a more balanced life."

Patrick: age sixty-one, research director

"I've been celibate for two and a half years, since my divorce. I was married for twenty years, and we have four children. I would say that the main desires I have in my life are the pursuit of my work and taking care of my family. My time is very precious to me—to pursue a woman to have an affair or to have a future commitment—these are not part of my interests right now. I have no desire to be remarried.

Several years before the divorce, my time became very limited. My work had become more and more absorbing and also enjoyable. We had an excellent sex life together, but my wife wanted more time together—certainly a natural desire for her but a difficult one for me. I seemed to want less of a sexual relationship than she did—it didn't seem to be spontaneous in light of our limited time together. The real reasons for our divorce were not problems of sex but problems of attention—how much I could give to my wife, how much to our children, how much to my work and all the people involved there. This situation hasn't changed much since the divorce.

I consider my sex life to be "normal." I've had sexual experiences for forty years. I think I had average sexual desires, although not much expression in fantasy. My fantasies now aren't generally sexual either. I feel that at this point, the intensity of needs and physiological functioning are over and truthfully, I'm glad about it. I don't see that being sexual all your life is either necessary or desirable.

I grew up in a strict Lutheran-Catholic environment. Perhaps I would have been more familiar with and, therefore, more sexual with women if I had had a less religious upbringing, but I don't think so. For one thing, I was a training athlete throughout my youth, and I think I expanded my energies towards a commitment to sports and competition. My first sexual encounter was with my first wife when I was twenty-one. I went into the service at age twenty-four and was celibate for three years during the war, but I didn't mind. My attention was in a different place than on sexuality at the time. But I guess celibacy was never as difficult for me as it may be for other men. I really don't know.

I do enjoy the company of women a great deal. I am

attracted to them and they to me. But since I'm not really wanting to pursue a sex-based relationship, I try not to make myself available. I don't seek sex, but I enjoy playing sports with women and working with them in a comfortable, friendly way. When I have some extra time, I play tennis and golf and usually jog about five miles a day if possible. These activities are made more enjoyable by the company of women.

My basic theory about sex is that the intensity of desire changes as the attention changes and vice versa. At first, male attention is almost entirely on sex. It seems to be a major way men prove themselves. But as you get older, you've experienced so much sex in the past, and you know what it is. Your attention then may shift to other things. I'm at least a semi-mature creature and don't seem to want to run around looking for sex. I live with a certain amount of ease and peace. For me, sex was deeply connected with family life and children. At this time, sex is not very interesting to me, and I would be forcing it if I tried to make it more important than it is. So celibacy seems very natural. There is really no other choice. And I'm happy with it.''

Don: age thirty-two, store manager

"Two years ago, I decided to be celibate just to see what my relations with women would be like. At the time, they weren't very satisfactory. I kept sleeping with women in hopes of falling in love with them. I was forever looking for the "ideal" woman who would share all my hopes and dreams and look at things the same way as I did. I guess I was very afraid of being open with women. I didn't want them to be different from me because I was too insecure to accept women as different. If I slept with a woman who didn't share the same values, I'd almost have to sit and stare at the wall for two days in order to recover. But since I was pretty obsessed with sex, I slept with anyone I could, not usually going further than sex in the relationship.

I was celibate for about eight months. I just decided it was a good way to break a bad pattern of behavior. At first, I noticed a kind of irritability from not having sex regularly, but then I noticed a kind of heightened perception in understanding people. I began to "see" women as people, maybe for the first time. A funny thing was that women became inordinately attracted to me, perhaps because I gave them a certain kind of attention that was really more powerful than sexual attention.

As I became more relaxed about being with women, I started to have sexual relations again, but they seemed less important even though more comfortable and enjoyable. I didn't need to prove myself through sex. Now, sex is not the number one desire nor my main interest with women. I feel more even with them. I still desire a deep mutuality with a woman, and I feel that this goal is more possible now."

The
Celibate Woman

A SHORT
SEXUAL HISTORY

5 Throughout most of world history, in ancient Persia, in China (even until this century), in India, Greece—in all the highest civilizations—women have remained uneducated. Bertrand Russell notes:

> In most civilized communities, women have been denied almost all experience of the world and of affairs. They have been kept artificially stupid and, therefore, uninteresting. From Plato's dialogues one derives an impression that he and his friends regarded men as the only proper objects of serious love. This is not to be wondered at when one considers that all the matters in which they were interested were completely closed to respectable Athenian women.[1]

This lack of education is reflected in the lack of sexual knowledge accorded women. Not only were women kept "noneducated," they were also kept "nonsexual." Every so often in history this was not the case but in general, women's sexuality was viewed only in terms of their ability to elicit male sexual response.

Women have been credited historically with every vice and with every virtue. Woman has moved from the sexual status of low-down temptress to unearthly saint and back again. Many religions have imbued women with all sorts of sexual powers and then taken them away. A striking example of this dichotomy occurs in Christianity, where one woman (Eve) is the cause of original sin and the fall from grace, and another woman (Mary) is the inspiration for the purity of all devouts—including the celibates of the priesthood.

Historically, women were dependent socially and economically but not sexually upon men. They were not sexually dependent because they were not considered "sexual." Some researchers have speculated that this was because female sexual response was unnecessary for reproduction. Only male orgasm was required, and therefore women's only real sexual function was to serve as what Masters and Johnson have indelicately called "seminal receptacles."

As female sexuality was never even considered apart from marital obligations and childbearing functions, women were not attentive to their own sexual desires—nor was male attention put upon their needs. As a result, women learned either not to be sexual or never learned to *be* sexual.

It is interesting that although recent research in sexuality has revealed women's great sexual capacity (an orgasmic capacity demonstrated to be much greater than men's), there is no evidence that women experienced what we call sexual frustration. Not knowing their own sexual natures and not called upon to have sexual lives, they were apparently not disappointed. Author Barbara Seaman maintains that those Victorian women who were "totally unaroused" sexually were nonetheless often in love with their husbands for a lifetime and "were not consciously frustrated."

As women obtained their long-overdue education, they became more knowledgeable about all aspects of life, including their own sexuality. But when women's sexuality was finally acknowledged in America and England a century ago, a great attempt was made to continue to keep women nonsexual. Thus the Victorian era became synonymous

with sexual repression. It was a time in which sexual innocence gave way to sexual knowledge, but in the process
both the innocence and the knowledge became falsified.

In an effort to deny what was considered the shocking
reality of female sexuality, Victorian society put forth some
amazing distortions. Men were said to have "bestial" sexual needs and women had to be protected from them. In
fact, Victorian women held a widespread belief that they
were morally superior to men *because* they experienced less
pleasure in sex. Women were supposed to be completely
blind to their own feelings, negating any indication of possible compliance on their part. This extreme denial was so
severe that "good" women could not even accept their own
organic structures lest the truth be known. It is reported
that many women died rather than undergo much-needed
gynecological examinations and admit to their own sexual
organs. Even as recently as fifty years ago, it was illegal in
England to state in print that a wife can and should derive
pleasure from sexual activities.

Under these conditions, it is not surprising that sex
took on a huge, unnatural significance—far more powerful
in such a repressive era than in times when sex is quietly
accepted for its own specific role in the culture.

To counteract this absurd distortion came Freud and
his theory of sexuality, which represented neurotic and
normal behaviors as based on degrees of repression and
sublimation of sexuality. Freud's remarkable insights
brought about a much-needed opening of awareness and
acceptance of human sexuality, but at the same time
created other distortions. The unfortunate result of Freud's
view of his own age led more recent societies to overvalue
sex and its role in human development.

One particular aspect of Freud's theory that was embraced until a decade ago was the biological model of female
sexuality which erroneously defined women's capabilities
based on incomplete physiological knowledge. This information was only recently corrected through the work of Dr.
Mary Jane Sherfey, Masters and Johnson, and others. And

as the result of this prolonged misunderstanding, women who were sexually normal were taught that they were not. This was not as painful to women in the days when they were appreciated for their nonsexual functions during the times when marriage and motherhood were glorified. But as that emphasis shifted and sexual and romantic love became the standard for a woman's social success, the seeming inability to behave as a sexually "normal" woman was a great psychological blow to many women, especially at a time when they were supposed to feel sexually liberated.

This led to a particularly narrow view of women's psychology, perhaps best summarized in the statement by Percival Symonds that "Women seek love experiences for the restoration of wounded self-esteem." When the only acceptable role for women to play is a sexual-romantic one and when a woman's worth is based on sexual attractiveness, it is no wonder that women who thought that there was something wrong with them sexually experienced a great deal of social insecurity.

And this transition from being nonsexual to being "abnormal" was no doubt a key factor in the decision of many women finally to determine their own sexuality for themselves and evaluate their sexual needs in terms that men never used—related to independence and self-worth. This in turn led some women to see their sexuality in a somewhat biased fashion—as a key to personality and as a means for personal liberation. During the 1960s, this most likely served as a spur to the women's movement, which attempted to sort out the confused female experience of the sexual revolution.

WOMEN'S REACTION TO
THE SEXUAL REVOLUTION

Most women found the effect of the sexual revolution a mixed blessing. There have been, of course, various responses by women to what has been seen alternatively as a more liberalized freeing of sexuality to a more restrictive mechanizing of sex-as-orgasm. There are some women who have embraced the social freedom of unattached sexuality by mimicking some men who want to, if not "have it all" at least "do it all." Reflecting on this indiscriminate behavior, Barbara Seaman wrote: "It has long been argued that it takes three generations to make a natural gentleman. Perhaps by the same token, it will take three generations to make a naturally-liberated woman. Some of the girls who discover sexual freedom are a bit like *nouveau riche* males, at first, expending their wealth universally and with very questionable taste."[2]

Other women have applauded some of the results—particularly the informational benefits—but continue to feel uncomfortable regarding their sexuality. A precarious balance seems to be required: (1) A woman must be careful not to threaten men by being too open about wanting sex and must continue to allow herself to be "seduced" into something she presumably wants anyway and (2) a woman must be ready and available and willing to have sex in order to not be considered hung-up, antisocial, or repressed. Repression is the worst sin of all. A startling example of this modern concern was reported by newscaster David Brinkley on the NBC Evening News in May, 1979: one in five American male doctors questioned stated that they believe it is helpful for their female patients if they have erotic contact with them.

The Female Orgasm
The major emphasis to emerge from the sexual revolution was the female orgasm and the achievement thereof; in many ways this further tightened the already restrictive focus of lovemaking. It became the prime concern not only for women but for men.

As a result, there is some regret for the loss of the less goal-oriented days. As one woman wrote in response to Shere Hite's questionnaire, "The rare times when sex was a tool for healing, or emotional relating when extra warmth and intimacy were needed, orgasm was unnecessary. Also, before I learned how to have an orgasm, sex was a service of intimacy to my partner. . . ."

Anthropologist Margaret Mead observed that female orgasm is not a problem in most primitive cultures, where men are trained to bring women to orgasm as part of their social responsibilities. But in our culture until very recently, while male orgasms were thought of as inevitable, female orgasms were depicted as rare, mysterious, and difficult to achieve, requiring hard work and concentration. Today a woman is advised to take responsibility for her orgasms and her task-orientation can be just as grim as any of woman's "traditional" chores—with perhaps a more pleasurable but not much more fulfilling ending than a clean house.

Whereas before, women were content to enjoy sex with or without orgasm, now they too (along with men) have been taught to view orgasm as the goal of lovemaking: Taking their cues from male sexual habits, some women now feel they deserve what they give in return. In extreme instances, the female orgasm has become a very political issue: EQUAL PAY FOR EQUAL WORK or AN ORGASM FOR AN ORGASM. This attitude can be readily traced to the deprivation many women experienced in unsatisfactory sexual relationships. Yet it also serves to narrow women's sexuality to the same limited framework which has been the restrictive focus in male sexuality, prohibiting deeper and fuller experiences to occur.

Fortunately, most women have begun to see the limiting effects of orgasm-oriented love and are revealing what they really enjoy, even if it means reversing some of the so-called advances they have gained.

"Women like sex," writes Shere Hite, "more for the feelings involved than for the purely physical sensations of intercourse per se." Her survey showed that sex is considered important to women because of the intimacy and closeness it provides with another human being—as a way of showing deepest love. This is also why women like sexual intercourse specifically, because of the closeness (not necessarily the sexuality) of the physical expression of love. Sex is also considered important because women see it as a way to establish their feelings of security and desirability and as an affirmation of self-worth. Sex is also a time of giving pleasure to a partner—a time of trust and surrender in love.

Sex is a conditioned response. For a woman it can be something familiar, something that makes a woman feel "official," "real." Women have been found to respond to sexual activity based on what they have been taught about sex. For women as well as for men, sex is a learned response, even if new learning replaces old lessons. If a woman is taught that sex occurs as foreplay, sexual intercourse, male ejaculation, this is what she will hold sex to be and will feel "wrong" with another sequence or set of activities. If a woman is taught to view sexual intercourse or the reproductive model of sexuality as exploitive and the female orgasm as the only justifiable reason to engage in sexual activity, this is what sex will be for her and anything else will seem false.

There is little doubt that their nonsexual history still very much affects the thinking of many women. One indicator of this is the difference between men's and women's fantasy lives. Whereas men tend to fantasize more when they are not involved in a relationship, women have been found to think about and fantasize much less about sex when they are not involved. And whereas men will fantasize in order to become aroused, women fantasize in order to become "unaroused"—to achieve orgasm. Strictly physical fantasies focused on the ongoing sexual experience itself are most common. It is also interesting that very few women have any basis for connecting their sexual feelings with other aspects of their lives and have not been found to fantasize using more universal or spiritual images.

The Sexuality of Older Women

According to Wade, Seaman, and others, most women tend to have increased sexual desires after the age of thirty. This eroticism is said to increase and continue through menopause and after, until about age sixty-five, when a slow decline in sexual interest begins. Dr. Helen Kaplan explains: "While some women report a decrease in sexual desire, many women actually feel an increase in erotic appetite during the menopausal years. . . . From a purely physiologic standpoint, libido should theoretically increase at menopause, because the action of woman's androgens . . is now unopposed by estrogen."[3]

Dr. Mary Jane Sherfey also found that women become more sexual as they get older, perhaps because of the development of a larger system of veins in the genital area. So it seems that although older women are not capable of reproductive sex, they are more capable than ever of experiencing sexual pleasure. Shere Hite writes that women should think of their bodies as sexually capable for a lifetime but with reproductive capacities limited to a certain number of years in the middle

A one older woman reported to Hite: "I think that men are conned into believing that [sex] decreases in age for them I don't think it decreases drastically for anyone, especially for women. My best sexual experiences are coming out of maturity and self-confidence."

Given the fact that older women are sexual women and, like men, have the ability to be sexual all their lives, a similar confusion has developed. Like older men, older women in our society are put in a most difficult situation that demands an impossible integration of physical and social requirements. On the one hand, women are exploding the myth that older women are not sexual by continuing their sexual lives well into their seventies and eighties. On the other hand, women are beginning to feel a certain social obligation to be sexual at a time in their lives when other kinds of experiences may fascinate them more. The social pressure to maintain sexual activity in their later years is less of a problem for women than for men, primarily because for so many hundreds of years, older women's sexuality was not welcomed. But it is growing.

Ironically, in an effort to be fair to older women, writers like Shere Hite seem to put more pressure on older women to be sexually liberated than they do on younger women. But it seems that the dignity and level of experience of age should permit both older women and older men to be at last free of the narrowness of sexually based social acceptance.

Older women have the option to be sexual or celibate, based not on what they "should" be having in the way of sexual lives, but on their actual interest. For, given the physical possibilities, any woman can have sex at any age, but not all women want to. A woman may feel she needs to continue to prove her sexual attractiveness whether she wants sex or not, but this is a decision she must make. Not all women need that reassurance.

Many older women do not have the opportunity to be sexually involved, especially if they are divorced or widowed. To be put into the position of feeling deprived because they are not leading full sexual lives is a psychological burden most older women could do without. The real sense of worth and fulfillment can never come from sex anyway: the older woman misses the value of her development if she allows her sexual life to represent her at age seventy. Sure, she has sexual feelings and desires—and so do five-year-old girls. But it is better not to mistake this one small avenue of self-expression for the power of womanhood at any age.

Women's Sexual Desire

Perhaps because of their short history of overt sexuality, women seem to be more flexible about sexual desire than do men. For the most part, women have learned to accommodate their sexuality to the situation. This works two ways: On the one side, women don't have to be convinced to have sex. As one woman said, "The reason why so-called seduction practices work is that [a woman] is simply an erotic being in her own right, and with the proper attention and stimulation, she'll be at a point where she'd rather have sex than anything."[4]

On the other side, most women do not report a regular sexual appetite. Hite found that "the appetite for sex with another person became really intense only in relation to desire for a specific person." Many of her respondents reported that when sex wasn't available (when they were not involved in a specific relationship), they tended not to want sex. Her conclusion: "The less you have it, the less you want it."

MOVING TOWARD CELIBACY

Only recently have women begun to evaluate their own sexuality in light of their own desires and goals. Until now, women have been told how they should think about sex. Some women have noted that whereas before the revolution they were advised to have sex rarely, now they're advised to have it regularly.

It is apparent that women are not as interested in sex today as they think they ought to be. What women seem to be most interested in—fulfillment in relationships and personal growth—has not been particularly advanced by the revolution in sexual attitudes. Women are finding that "good sex and plenty of it" does not bring the fulfillment they are seeking. As a result of the new attitudes, women know they can have orgasms but are now expected to have them and enjoy them more than other aspects of their lives. The pressure to have sex, orgasms, and to say they enjoy it has created in women a new set of concerns that only seem to replace, not to do away with, the problems they faced before the revolution.

"If I go for long without sex, my desires drop ridiculously, which worries me. I start to wonder if something is 'wrong' with me, which makes me feel obligated to have sex."[5]

The most difficult social dilemma most women face today is the social pressure to be sexual even when they do not want to be. The pressure comes not only from interested men but from social arbiters of "normal" living—the "experts"—as well as from other women who want support for their own sexual activities.

Just as it was a near-social impossibility for a woman to say yes when all society told her to say no, now the very opposite situation confronts her. This confusion is heightened by the accompanying confusion of social roles women must learn anew. Despite their new knowledge, most women do not want to lose men's love and feel that sex is the only way to assure it. (This situation is further compounded by the pressure not only to have sex freely but also to have an orgasm every time.)

Learning to say no is not that easy for most women, but in the process of making that choice, a woman begins to overcome not only social but personal limitations. As psychoanalyst June Singer writes:

> In the process of asserting herself and saying *no* for the first time, a woman may learn a great deal. If she is sufficiently committed to the task of increasing her level of consciousness, she may discover that not all of the opposition is outside, not all is coming from men, not all is coming from the world. Much of it is internal. Woman is bound, at least to some degree, because she allows herself to be bound, and often in the name of love. It is a stage that many creative women have to go through.[6]

And, according to the observations of Masters and Johnson, "A woman cannot be sexually emancipated without first becoming personally emancipated."

What Women Really Want

Women want to love and be loved and are apparently more open about that desire than are men. Despite their ability to be more sexual than men, at least in their capacity for multiple orgasms, women in general continue to prefer the emotional to the sexual aspects of their relationships.* Consequently, given a choice between good sex and good emotional contact, women far prefer the latter—the sharing, intimacy, touching, and tenderness.

Touch is very important to most humans, and few people in our society get enough of it. Yet touching is most often used to prepare for sexual activity and not enjoyed simply for its own pleasure. Most women want to touch and be touched, independent of sex.

For many women, the emotional satisfactions of intimacy with or without sex are the essence of making love. Physical closeness without physical sex is something that women tend to enjoy and quite a few actually prefer to the experience of orgasm because it incorporates so many of the subtleties of love and romance.

Orgasm of the Heart

Closer to the experience women describe as most desirable is a more intimate kind of "orgasm" or melting of feeling, which sometimes occurs during sex and sometimes does not. Shere Hite reports that women in general are seeking emotional orgasms, peaks of love, far more than they are looking for great physical orgasms. It seems likely that men too are searching for those experiences that melt the heart. A physical orgasm, whether genitally localized or enjoyed more generally throughout the body, is only as moving as the feelings accompanying it. When the heart has "an orgasm," when it melts in the ecstasy of love and the fullness of tender feelings, this is a truly unforgettable experience. And while the sensation of physical orgasm leaves the body

*This preference is borne out in Masters and Johnson's research, where it was found that although female orgasm through masturbation is usually more intense and occurs with much greater frequency than orgasm through intercourse, most women prefer the closeness of intercourse because the emotional component of sexuality is far more important to them than orgasm.

within seconds, the feelings of the emotional orgasm are often maintained at a delicate level of pleasure to be enjoyed in waves of love again and again with a look or a smile.

Because they have had much more experience with nonorgasmic or non-goal-oriented sex, it is likely that women are more experienced in the level of lovemaking that has been called "transcendent" sex or "unboundedness" occurring during sexual activity. Without orgasm, sexuality has the opportunity to become diffused into a more subtle exchange of energy and love. And women who have experienced this kind of sexuality are actually enjoying a level of experience which has been generally reserved for the practitioners of the highest art of lovemaking in many cultures. But a woman (or a man) can only experience this kind of diffused expansion if she (or he) is not misled into thinking that only sex with orgasm quickly achieved is valid lovemaking.

Celibacy and Today's Women

> This new chastity is more challenging, because the pressure from the culture is very strong *not* to be chaste. Most women feel about as satisfied after casual, perfunctory sex as they do after a sneeze. There's a momentary release of tension, but no real involvement. What I think we are seeing here among this newly celibate group is a backlash against the sexual revolution.[7]
> —DR. JOYCE BROTHERS

Most women are celibate or without sex for extensive periods of time in their lives—whether as a youngster or as a widow, as a single woman, a divorcee or even during marriage for a variety of reasons. But the tendency on the part of many women is to disregard these times and to consider only the times of sexuality to be valuable. In *The Hite Report*, although most women reported that they have had frequent times of celibacy and a large number felt they could easily be celibate, less than 1 percent considered themselves celibate. Many women, it seems, cannot see that being celibate has any redeeming social value in their lives and, consequently, would not admit to it. Yet one well-known man who practiced celibacy, interviewed on the *David Susskind Show* in 1978, noted that of the women he knew who were comfortable telling him about their sexuality, at least 75 percent wanted to be celibate but did not feel they could be, since most men expected women to be sexual. This attitude is understandable if viewed historically; it is safe to say that most women with a long history of confused sexuality would naturally be wary of any sign of the "re-repression" of their sexuality. What they fail to see is that at another level, being celibate by choice is more liberating than being sexual by demand.

Most studies on women report that as women finally become aware of their habit behaviors, dependencies, and low self-esteem, they begin to reject sexual relationships which are not valuable for them. They recognize how men and women can get into binding behaviors that are mutually restrictive. They seek to develop entirely new kinds of relationships based on less inhibiting ways of relating. For a number of women, celibacy offers that opportunity.

Becoming celibate for a time is not a closing off but an opening up. It allows women to break old patterns of behavior, dependencies, limits. Women find that becoming celibate enables them to experience a greater degree of self-sufficiency and freedom while at the same time offering a chance to explore new dimensions in relationships. It can be a time to free a woman from the frantic nature of sexual activity and its narrow focus. And it can be a time to sort out feelings about a particular relationship without the mask of sex—to allow the deepening of a love relationship to occur in a more unbounded field.

Women who practice celibacy have experiences that range from their good feelings about finally "taking charge of their own bodies" to experiences of increased energy in all aspects of their lives to feelings of peacefulness, settledness, "centeredness," and the development and growth of spiritual life.

Becoming Celibate

Here are excerpts from interviews with a number of women who have had periods of celibacy throughout their adult life. In general, they tended to regard being celibate in a very positive way—not as a social disability but as a time for improving relationships, a time to evaluate one's sexuality and as a means for personal independence.

"Because I need to feel a *real* commitment to a man in order to have an ongoing sexual relationship, I am currently celibate. I used to have sex often, but I found that without commitment, sex doesn't get any better than the first time you have it with someone.The first time always seems the best and after that, less and less of that anticipation and openness is there—and then you spend later times trying to recapture it."

"While I am celibate, I am able to experience my friends in the present—more for *all* of who they are than just a part of them. The intimacy is very deep when there is no goal like orgasm. My giving to them isn't held back for some future time when they 'deserve' it—like saving your energy for right before the finish line."

"It is a true test of men. If, when they find out I'm celibate, they don't immediately lose interest, then they're usually interested in meeting me in some more important place, and right away we've got more going for us than if we'd gotten off at the first bedroom along the way."

"When I was celibate [last year], I found I had much more of *me* to invest in my work. At times, I felt less social than I do when I am not being celibate, but at other times I felt that my work was really more rewarding than any relationship I could have had at the time and that I was being really honest with myself to accept what other people saw as slightly 'wrong'—to be more interested in what I was doing on my job than in having a sexual/social life. I think many women committed to a career must go through this from time to time."

"Better than sex plus orgasm, I have always preferred to touch and be touched on a much more relaxed un-pressured basis, always staying in tune with myself throughout the physical exchange. So I am celibate most of the time and yet maintain an active 'touch' life when I can find people to appreciate that experience as much as I do. Actually, it was a man who taught me the value of touching. I'm not frustrated because I get a lot of emotional nourish-ment this way, and I save sex for the few people who really capture my heart."

"Interestingly, since I've been celibate, my sexual interest has stayed about the same, but I'm not at all frus-trated in that I have the right to decide how to use the energy that sexuality engenders in me. It's really a great resource."

"This may surprise you, but I like being celibate be-cause I'm not wary about going out any more. *I* decide if I like a guy without sex confusing the issue. Before, even though I was never really hung up sexually, there was al-ways this fear that I wouldn't measure up to a man's expec-tations of me sexually. This was most gruesome when I wouldn't even know the man, and I'd be getting ready to be 'judged' on my physical attributes by a total stranger. And you wonder why women who are so against beauty pageants and the like are willing to go through similar an-guish. Now, I feel in control and happy with my self and, truthfully, a lot closer to men."

Celibacy as a Means to Sexual Liberation

As they have gained awareness of their own sexual inde-pendence, women are becoming aware that being sexually independent does not mean being independent from *men* but being independent from *sex*. Choosing to be with someone sexually means two things: (1) that one has chosen to be with that person and (2) that one has chosen to be sexual. Men don't limit women's fulfillment sexually—it is sex that is limited, far more so than being with another person with all other channels of communication beginning to open.

If a woman chooses celibacy as a protest against men, it loses its value as a mode of learning about the nonsexual sharing between two people. It is clear to people who have experienced celibacy and continued to have relationships that these relationships expand immeasurably without the restrictive nature of socially defined sexual expression as the height of value in romantic relationships.

The kind of self-expansion and related social expansion which times of celibacy can bring come about through the softening effects of unrestricted love diffused throughout all experience. And celibacy for a woman is not good if it is not generous. It must not be repression or refusal but a natural coinciding of her behavior with the most loving dimensions of her nature to enable her to enjoy new horizons in her life.

Women's Liberation:
Freedom from Sex and Beyond

As women's sexual identity has shifted from childbearer to sex "object" in response to the societal shift from the family emphasis to the focus on individual love relationships, women find themselves in a very difficult social position. What was meant to be progressive and liberating for them—the freedom implied by the sexual revolution—may have forced a further restriction on their social lives. This is partly because the role of a sex object or even a sex "subject" is far more limited than even the role of a wife and mother in the opportunity for growth. The mystery of the orgasm has been solved, but the real nature of being a woman remains even more hidden. As Diana Trilling has said:

> I know any number of borderline psychotics who are having perfectly fine sexual lives, in the sense that they have or-

gasms, lots of them, if that's what you define it by. . . .

I think women are being liberated to be a mess. They have the right to be as much of a mess as men, they really do. But I do think we'd all be a lot better off if we didn't think that to be liberated to be a mess is somehow a fulfillment of our femininity.[8]

FIVE CELIBATE WOMEN

Evie: age twenty-six, dancer

"I have been celibate for about a year. My main reason for becoming celibate was that I wanted a way of really seeing where I was at with a man and where he was at with me. I have really wanted to be appreciated by men for the more sweet, giving and innocent aspects of my personality. If I go out with a man now, and he knows that I'm celibate, I assume that he is with me because he is interested in me not as a sexual person but for other reasons. In the beginning, I remember thinking to myself, "How many dates will it take until he loses interest?"

I've always wanted to be more intimate in my relationships than the sexual kind of intimacy permits. The activity of sex does not seem to promote the kind of intimacy I am looking for. It's funny because I am actually very sexual, not at all asexual, but being celibate has given me a new way to investigate my feelings and to appreciate myself more. And my relations with men have deepened. I am not as anxious as I was when sex was *the* criterion for a successful relationship, and I feel a great deal more *myself*—like this is who I really am—I am not going to fool you with sex. I have met some truly affectionate men who make me feel very womanly and nurtured and appreciated even without "the reward" of sex. I love to touch and be touched and this has certainly not diminished but has become even more meaningful.

In other aspects of my life, I notice a kind of strength, and I really think it's from being celibate even though I know that sounds medieval. In my dance, I have more energy, and I am less fearful and uncertain. I feel like I have entered another dimension in my dancing coming from a sweeter, purer place in my heart.

Preoccupation with sex has definitely diminished. I used to think about it all the time. Even masturbation, something I never thought I'd ever want to stop, has somehow dropped off automatically.

I think I'll be married one day, and when I am, I don't want to be celibate in the marriage unless it's totally natural for both of us. But I do see myself being comfortably celibate until I'm married or until I am with a man in a very complete way on all other levels.''

Alexandra: age forty-two, counselor

''I've been celibate for about four years. When I first thought of being celibate, I didn't even know the word 'celibacy.' I had been going out a lot, having sex, feeling drained, outflowing, scattered, as though I were giving myself away. The physical acts of sex were fine, enjoyable, but I rarely felt energized from the experience.

I have been married twice and was divorced five years ago from my second husband. We had a relatively good sex life, but once the orgasm was over, I always had an after-feeling of not being ''whole.'' My lack of interest in sex was an issue in the marriage. It became a major issue at the time of divorce, but I think the real problems in our marriage were covered up by our focus on the sex issue.

I don't think sex is good or bad. I think of sex as the frosting on the cake. You can have it or not. If you have a good cake, you don't need frosting. And sometimes frosting overpowers a good cake or is used to cover up a bad one.

Sex has never been the part of my life that most intrigued me. But my sexuality has always been very prominent in my awareness. My sexual chronology started early. I began menstruating when I was eight—I haven't grown physically much since fifth grade. I started having sex with boys when I was a freshman in high school. But I spent the six years before going through my sexual growth pretty much alone and building up a lot of expectation and fantasy about sex. I would watch my body change and observe how I felt. Not surprisingly, my first sexual experiences were pretty disillusioning. But they got better, and I've enjoyed a very pleasurable sex life. But now I feel as though I've been through the entire cycle of sexuality already. And I definitely feel that to prolong my sexual life until I'm sixty or seventy would be an imposition on the rest of my life.

Since I've become celibate, I *use* my sexual feelings instead of giving them away. I watch the feeling; I get into it. I love how I feel in this quiet way. I don't try to avoid feeling sexual—rather, I play with the feeling. But I don't let it control me. I really don't like being run by anything—I especially don't enjoy being manipulated by a physical feeling. Most people don't, but when they feel sexual, they let the feeling take over to the point where all they can do is try and get rid of it and aim for release. Where many seem to run away from their sexuality, I *feel* my sexual feelings without trying to quickly minimize them through having sex.

I sometimes have visualized sex activity as a leak in my energy pipe. If you stop the drip, you get a continuous even flow of energy without diverting it into a wasteful stream. For this reason, I don't masturbate, because my energy feels too precious to me.

As a counselor, I help people get in touch with their feelings and fully live their experiences. Far beyond sex, what people seem to need most is "naked" *intimacy*; many people I see never really relate "unclothed" with their guard down to anyone, not even to their spouses.

I never advise anyone to be celibate. Most people I counsel would need a much greater support system for being celibate than is currently available within our social structure. Also, I believe that a person has to be in touch with his or her sexuality and not be frightened of it before becoming celibate. Otherwise, they may be very divided and feel unintegrated. I do have one friend who is also celibate, and I support her in this.

I've experienced some interesting benefits from becoming celibate. I lost forty pounds in the first six months. When actively sexual, I had experienced my body as round, from a constant search outward for nurturance through sex. On becoming celibate, I seemed to "pull in" my energy; in turn, my body became stronger and more upright in my mind. The weight just dropped off. Another thing that happened is that I'm much more able to be physical with others. I'm much more present in the experience instead of waiting for "the next step." I feel less restricted, less threatened, more spontaneous.

I feel more pure, more whole, more true to myself and much more able to love deeply. My sexual energy seems to flow easily into my feelings of love. I really enjoy giving to others because, unlike sex, it doesn't end and there is no need for a mutual payoff. I used to go outward with my energy both sexually and socially. Now I go inward, and I believe that is why my ability to love has deepened.

Being celibate hasn't meant not being with men. Quite the contrary—I don't "date" a lot, but I have a great many male friends, one in particular. Recently, after a movie, he brought me home, took me upstairs, undressed me and gave me a full body massage. Afterwards, he said, "I feel closer to you now than if we had had sex together." It was a very intimate expression of love for both of us.

Almost everyone I know is sexually-oriented, but most men seem to respect my desire to be celibate. I generally let them know if I'm asked out. They either don't mind, are intrigued, or feel challenged. If the latter happens, we go our separate ways. I seem to get the most negativity about celibacy from other women. I have the feeling that every woman wants to be celibate from time to time, but few are strong enough to resist the social pressure. There is a lot of resentment for this reason. I think one has to be ready to be celibate just as one has to be ready to be sexual. But you have to be able to choose for yourself based on your own needs. I can't advise it for everyone.''

Roxanne: age fifty-four, fashion coordinator

[*Roxanne has been married three times since age twenty, has one daughter, and has been divorced for the past twelve years. She estimates that she has had seven affairs thus far in her life, only one since her last divorce.*]

"My being celibate is a constant choice with every man I meet. I just can't hop into bed. I'm very choosy. I'm all for sex, but it's got to be part of a bigger thing. By itself, sex doesn't mean much. There's got to be a depth of relationship. I had one sexual affair since my last divorce. I thought it would be "good for me"—that's what everyone says. But it didn't work. I have to have that deep involvement. So I'm celibate.

I seem to be different from other women—particularly the younger ones who tend to treat sex more casually and more on its own. Celibacy partly represents my self-esteem, I guess; I'm celibate because I want more than sex, and I can't compromise. I think it's made me stronger.

I have always enjoyed sex a great deal. It's very pleasurable. And I have a lot of sexual energy. So I've learned to use it in nonsexual ways. Rather than worrying about what to do about feeling sexual, I use my sexual energy to get things done. I look at it as a positive energy flow that's all mine. I can bring it to any part of my body; I use it in my arms and legs for running or lifting. I bring it to my mind for talking, for learning. So, for me, being celibate doesn't mean I'm blocking my sexuality. I use it and it keeps me strong, dynamic, youthful. I think sex keeps you young, but you don't have to express your sexuality in just one way. You can use it anyway you want. Many women my age are not that interested in sex, particularly in their marriages. It's become dull. But they feel they *should* be sexual, so they feel guilty unless they're "with it." They have sex, but they don't enjoy their sexuality. They perform, but they are blocked. I'm celibate, and I use and enjoy my sexuality without being blocked. It's a funny paradox.

I'm an artist, and my creative growth is very important to me. I realize that the biggest periods of growth in my life have come during periods of celibacy. It's a very tangible growth which affects my daily living. As a woman alone, I supply my own needs. I have to draw love and affection from many sources. Without a deep relationship, I have learned to feel love through music, through the visual arts. I feel enlivened through a book, sharing ideas. It seems that as I've grown older, I've developed a level of deep awareness and love which must be touched for me to grow further. If I'm not deeply touched in a relationship, it's less satisfying than reading a book which truly moves me. I'm celibate because I look for *that* level in a relationship."

Sarah: age thirty-five, professor of linguistics

"I have always enjoyed sex. I guess I am one of the minority of women who are so constructed that they can have orgasms during intercourse, and this has always been a great pleasure for me. I never realized how fortunate I was until all the recent information on women's sexuality came out. But because I've always found sexual pleasure to be an "easy" experience for me (there wasn't much for me to learn or do better), sex has never provided much of an opportunity for growth in me. If you enjoy it a lot, you experience it fully, and then you begin to see its limitations.

About two years ago, I made a conscious decision to be celibate. It seemed like a natural happening. I was finding that sex, although enjoyable, was binding. What I mean is that for sex to be meaningful, you have to have a commitment to your lover. If you are to be faithful, you are in a sense bound sexually to your lover. Bound in this way, you expect tremendous rewards for the boundary. Sex has to keep being great for you to keep being committed. That level of relating starts to dominate the relationship. Sex seems to keep you at one level of relating when you really feel like you want to soar with it. You get lost in the activity, and you end up being committed to sex rather than being committed to more freeing, more delicate, more subtle possibilities that you are yearning to experience.

I love physical warmth and find it wonderfully nourishing. I find I am comfortable in a sensual, nonsexual relationship where I am not bowled over and I am not depending on sex to relate to the other person. If I lose myself, my "center," then I am not really enjoying the momentary experience. I discovered this in a particular relationship with a man I deeply loved. When I could take pleasure in each moment, each moment was a great thing; but with a focus on orgasm, the future became more important than the present.

I also have found, by contrast to being celibate, that sex is fatiguing. I never really realized it, but I used to feel quite dull afterwards and not very open to the person I was with. Being celibate offers all sorts of advantages—I relate more fully, more receptively, I am more alert and attuned; each moment has meaning. I feel stronger, more self-sufficient but also more open to loving and being loved deeply. It's actually more sensual being celibate than being sexual. Maybe I should write *Memoirs of the Sensual Celibate!*"

Marla: age twenty-four, graphic artist

[*Marla was celibate for two years–from age twenty to twenty-two–following the death of her boyfriend. She is currently living with a man with whom she has a nearly celibate relationship.*]

"I guess you could call me a child of the "beat generation." My father is a jazz musician, my mother is a writer and has been a practicing Zen Buddhist for twenty-five years. My parents met in Paris in the fifties. But when I came along, I think they became more conservative. I was educated at Catholic parochial schools. I spent a good part of my teen years reading romantic novels. My parents never told me the "facts of life": I guess they assumed I already knew them. My education came out of these novels and from my peers, and I always knew I wanted to "save myself for love."

What I thought was love came when I was fifteen: I had my first sexual experiences, but they were not at all what I had expected from the romances. In fact, they were pretty boring and unappealing—very different from my fantasies.

When I was seventeen, I met Bill. As in the song: "He was a carpenter, and I was a lady." He didn't talk much— he was very intuitive and perceptive. He also had great stability, love, and contentment with life. He really opened up my emotions and my sexuality. We lived together for a year and a half and then he was killed in an accident.

After the initial shock wore off, with friends and family helping, I became quite reclusive. The expression "she grew up fast" applied to me. Sex became a very serious issue for me. I resolved to take it seriously because I felt that the kind of sexual experiences I wanted would have to come from a really deep love. I guess it might have been a kind of vow somehow to make up for the loss of Bill. But it wasn't difficult for me to be celibate; it was the only way I felt. I didn't feel depressed; I just felt inward.

I became a more serious person all around. This is when my work became very enjoyable and productive. I finished my degree in art and even had a successful exhibition of my work.

The longings I had were not sexual—they were on a more cosmic level. The needs I felt were for tenderness and someone to hold me. Even though everyone around me was very concerned with sex, my attention just wasn't on it. I felt it was a waste of time, and I saw how convoluted it had become. Most of my friends were older than me, but I felt older than them. I was lonely, but I was also aware of wanting to be alone.

I started working in L.A. as a graphic designer. I began to feel more open to being involved with a man. I remember thinking, "I'm ready."

When I met Roy, it was the first time in two years that I thought someone was even attractive. Neither one of us had had even a dating relationship for a long time, and we both had been celibate—he for a year, and I for two. Naturally, we were both shy and cautious, but in a week we knew that we were going to be together—even sexually.

Initially, we were very conscious of having sex—it was really intense. I was scared but excited—it was not at all casual. We were very respectful of our sexuality. After all, we had "saved it up," so to speak. And it was great at first—a very spiritual exchange. But what I found was that as we began to have more and more sexual experiences together, we stopped communicating in other ways. We kind of let our minds go and became noticeably less interesting, at least intellectually. It was like giving each other a sexual gift was all we had the energy to give. Sex inspires you to give your all. But you don't always feel like giving more.

It has become a funny kind of dichotomy between our minds and our bodies. Either our bodies *or* our minds are joined, but rarely both at once. I have found that when we have sex, it's usually when we haven't been as emotionally together. When we feel we are really joined, it's a level of intensity that's difficult to maintain, and sex always overpowers that feeling. If we have to be celibate in order to maintain that intensity, it's no sacrifice.

Nowadays we are celibate most of the time and perhaps have sex once a month. It's a very good balance for us, and I prefer the results in all the other aspects of our relationship."

Celibacy in Marriage:
Chastity begins at home

ONE IS NOT BORN to be married: marriage is, as they say, "an acquired taste." One learns how to be married by being married, by observing one's parents, or, today, by having marriage-like experiences before marriage or instead of marriage. And how we value marriage will depend on how we learn to be married. The mutual learning that occurs in marital relations and the levels of intimacy derived from that learning form the basis on which a marriage grows.

Much of the marital focus of the past decades has been the growth in sexual knowledge that has taken place in premarital and marital relations with regard to mutual needs and practices. A number of researchers have pointed out that men and women are very different in their sexuality, due in part to the different ways they experience sexual learning.

Learning to give pleasure to one's spouse thus requires an understanding of his or her needs and capabilities; this has been the value of the information revolution in sexuality. This knowledge has helped to prepare couples who may not otherwise have realized the differences in sexuality between men and women. On the surface, therefore, it would seem that the sexual revolution has mainly brought about the learning opportunity for more and better experiences in marriage. But in reality the new sexual emphasis in marriage seems to have created a more narrow and restrictive evaluation of marital success—one based almost entirely on sexual success. And as a possible consequence we are beginning to see a rapidly growing dissolution of marriage and family life.

In reflecting on the oft-quoted statistic that one out of every three marriages (now closer to one out of every two) ends in divorce, while we cannot blame "too much sex" alone for this complex phenomenon, still we canot help observing that this divorce rate has come about as sexual satisfaction has become more and more valued. It is more valued than any other criterion of "good" social behavior—including other aspects of marital satisfaction. And so, when we do not find sex up to one's newly acquired expectations within the structure of marriage, we are now taught that it must be found somewhere else—in some other relationship or social situation. And in this way marriage is sometimes regarded as an imposition or barrier to personal happiness, especially if that happiness is thought to be primarily gained through sexual activity.

SEX AS THE
MIRROR OF MARRIAGE

Most people realize that it is the quality of the love relationship that determines the quality of the sexual relationship, not the other way around. Yet this obvious understanding is often lost in the current overemphasis on sexual living.

It may be fair to say that in recent years there has been no greater pressure in a marriage than sexual performance. In our society, sex is the mirror of marriage. If their "sex life" is not experienced as profoundly fulfilling, a couple is taught to recognize that their marriage is failing.

As a result, some marriages are almost entirely sexually dependent; the partners use sex as the exclusive motivation for their expression of intimacy and their continued willingness to share their lives. Many of these couples also use sex to control each other—demanding sex as a service, giving it as a reward, or withholding it as a punishment. These sex-based marriages are very difficult to maintain, as one or both partners are often unable to sustain sexual interest intense enough to uphold the whole marriage.

Even in more balanced marriages where the focus is not so one-sided, the sexual concerns are often used as a psychological filter for all the marital concerns. In his study of modern sexuality commissioned by *Playboy*, Morton Hunt concluded that a marriage is going well if "the sex" is good. Then, he reasons, there is not much need for extramarital sex, and the couple can remain faithful to one another.

Sex is even used to qualify emotional success in marriage. Women who do not have orgasms during sex with their husbands come to see their husbands as undependable and have been found to have a greater fear of losing them than "sexually successful" women. Masters and Johnson have noted that almost all the marriage guides available center their guidance on the premise that sex is the best indicator of success or failure in a marriage. Thus, as H. J. Campbell observed, "The fact that sexual joy is supposed to be an unquestioned feature of successful marriage will inevitably cause each partner to consider the marriage void for this reason alone."

In the early part of this century, Dr. Arthur Gould wrote that *over*indulgence in sex is "without doubt the cause of more unhappy marriages than any other influence. . . . It is the very fact that before marriage these fluids were retained in the body that created the magnetism which made the man and the woman so attractive to each other." Without defending or arguing against the validity of this view, we can at least appreciate the fact that not so many years later, the opposite theory for marital discord is now widely upheld in our society. Without an abundance of high-quality sex, a marriage may be viewed as a failure or empty of meaning. *Under*indulgence in sex, therefore, is considered to be the reflection of an unhappy marriage.

P.S.: Your Marriage Is Failing

Steve, thirty-three, has been returning home after work each evening full of excitement about his current project. He is finally getting to write—a long-held desire he never thought would be fulfilled at work. The boss likes his style and wants to give more writing responsibilities to him. Steve's whole attention is with this new assignment; he takes pleasure in his work. As he polishes each sentence, his mind and creative juices become absorbed in the task.

The last thing on Steve's mind these days is sex.

Steve's wife, Mary, also thirty-three, has been doing a lot of reading lately. After work, she has returned home to the books on sex with all the latest research and teachings. Encouraged by what she has read, she has been doing some of the exercises and has discovered a great thing—her unlimited capacity for orgasm. Mary is thrilled and eager to share and explore this new dimension of her physical life with Steve, who has always been the more sexual of the two. Mary takes Steve's lack of interest in sex as a sure sign that their marriage is falling apart.

In the March 1978 *McCall's*, an article by Marcia Lasswell and Norman Lobsenz entitled "Making Love: The Subtle Art of Matching Moods" described the impossibility of finding perfection in the sexual encounter every time and how continued disappointments lead to eventual lack of sexual interest on the part of one or both partners. They reported that therapists see more and more couples who are disappointed with their sexual lives together—not so much disappointed in the actual lovemaking as in the lack of mutuality of interests and times of being "in the mood." Most couples were found to have high sexual expectations and were not interested in casual sex even within marriage.

To combat the possibility that their marriage is losing its sexual definition, some couples go to the extreme of sexual appointments on a regular basis. Lasswell and Lobsenz noted that couples who use a schedule to make "reservations" in advance are faced with a problem of "too high expectations." In other words, sexual experiences do not seem to be altogether fulfilling when couples expect to have them regularly. That is because they are verging on becoming "habits."

Habits tend to be repetitive and contrary to growth. Habits, as routine behaviors in relationships, have been found to reduce the expansive nature of love and render its growth inconsequential. If sex becomes a habit, it tends to lose its spontaneity and become not only routine but negative. If a couple says "We have sex every Thursday and Saturday," it is likely they have managed to routinize sex into a pattern not unlike the routine of housework. Sex out of habit performs a service and "sex-as-service rarely leads to sustained pleasure," observe Masters and Johnson.

Most married couples who feel that sexuality is a required part of marriage do get into a routine of sex, whether they want to or not. And that routine itself tends to make sex somewhat static or fixed or what Masters and Johnson call "goal-oriented." What is needed is the understanding that marital sex changes and cannot remain static if it is to be rewarding.

The basic kind of change in sexuality that will occur from time to time in a marriage is that one or both partners will become either more or less sexual. The current societal emphasis on sexuality has created a sexual bias that favors the *increase* in sexual activity in a marriage and, therefore, often condones looking outside the marriage for sexual satisfaction if just one partner seems to require it. If one or both partners become *less* sexually interested, this is not so well regarded and may be grounds for divorce.

But actually, the change toward lessening sexual activity may be indicative not of the failure of a marriage but of a higher-level relationship between the marital partners. It has been found that in the most successful, committed marriages, sexual response may indeed diminish in its localized expression—while changing into another kind of response.

Sexuality naturally changes in marriage over the months and years. And the change most frequently observed is the growth from a localized response to a more generalized response. As Masters and Johnson suggest, "Sex in a warm, emotionally-committed relationship may change in character and sexual response may become diffused after a while."

It is this *diffusion* of sexual response that many couples mistake for the *absence* of sexual response. And they begin to become very concerned that their marriage is losing its sexual orientation and, therefore, its value. What they may fail to recognize is that the essential direction of the growth of love generally progresses from the sexual experience to the higher expressions of love—that, in fact, as the sexual response in marriage becomes diffused, the opportunity for intimate love increases. As Dr. Helen Colton noted in *Sex after the Sexual Revolution*, "What is truly love may not even *begin* until that [sexual] tension abates."

As a marriage progresses and sexual experience and response change, it may be that one partner changes before the other. In the best marriages, these changes will be taken in stride by both, but if the changes are not acceptable to the other partner who is unprepared for a breaking down of the routine or an expansion of the boundaries, then a large communication gap will undoubtedly arise—such as "I'm into God and you're into *Leather*?!"

IS SEX NECESSARY
FOR MARITAL LOVE?

Only a few today would argue that marriage is necessary for sex; sex without marriage is now fairly respectable and even encouraged as a preliminary to marital commitment. But what about the opposite consideration—is sex necessary for marriage? There is the more provocative issue for our day.

Despite their mutual procreative function, sex and

marriage are necessarily separate experiences and separate commitments. As behaviorist Campbell reminds us, "Sex is not inextricably involved with marriage or any other social institution. It is simply a form of sensory pleasure-seeking." And in its separate status, sex is a voluntary act and remains voluntary even within marriage. This voluntary nature of sexual activity in humans is what changes the sexual experience from the purely physical to the symbolic or spiritual union. Every sexual act within marriage is thus freely chosen—not automatically experienced unconsciously out of habit but consciously chosen out of love. And if a couple chooses not to express their love sexually, because sexual expression is not interesting to them at a particular time, their decision can only favor their freedom to choose wisely for themselves in their desire to enhance the growth of love.

A number of researchers have asked: *Is* sex a crucial feature of marriage? Does a healthy marriage necessitate an ongoing sexual relationship? No, not necessarily. Lewis Terman, a pioneer in the study of marital happiness, concludes: "Our data do not confirm the view so often heard that the key to happiness in marriage is nearly always to be found in sexual compatibility." At the University of Pittsburgh, in a study of happy marriages, two marital therapists found that more than 90 percent of their respondents had a "less than perfect" sexual relationship, but very few thought it was a problem in their marriages. One-third of the women questioned were more or less uninterested in sex but still felt love for their husbands. Forty-seven percent of the couples had sexual intercourse on the average between two and four times a month; 8 percent reported having intercourse less than once a month, and 2 percent had no intercourse at all. The study concluded that sex is not a crucial part of a happy marriage.[1]

In *The Mirages of Marriage*, William Lederer and Don Jackson report that "there is considerable evidence that an individual's *perception* of the sexual relationship is more

related to marital satisfaction than the sexual act itself."
They contend that frustration from the lack of sex "stems
more from a feeling of deprivation than from pure physical
necessity," that men and women can "live without sex and
still stay healthy," as long as "the renunciation corresponds
to [their] emotional needs." They found that within a marriage, a couple who have satisfying and happy sexual experiences may well have sex *less* frequently than "an unhappy pair frantically experimenting for a solution to their
discord" and conclude that sex is in no way essential for a
successful marriage.

In the face of the obvious social pressure to define
successful marriage based on sexual criteria, it is somewhat
surprising to find that there is evidence pointing to the understanding that sex is *not* a requirement for a good marriage. What, then, has been the result of the sexual revolution in marriage? Superficially, it appeared to free couples to
enjoy *more* sex, but in fact, if one probes deeper, it may be
found that the sexual revolution may have, in effect, made
sex *less* important in marriage than before.

The Demystification of Sex
We can regard the effects of the revolution in sexual knowledge as providing a concrete reduction in sexual mystifica-
tion. Once sex has been demystified—known for what it
really is and the specifics of its boundaries—a couple is free
to experience the fullest nature of sex without the restraints
of ignorance. Then, if they see that they want something
more than sex can provide, they may move beyond those
boundaries spontaneously. If we think that we're missing
something, that something takes on a great importance, but
once its value is known, it no longer holds such hidden
fascination. Thus, in one sense, being free to be completely
sexual together enables a couple to be free *from* sexuality so
they may explore further horizons of the love relationship.

Most married couples have been taught that bringing
sexual "fulfillment" to their partner is the most intimate

contribution they could make to the marriage. But they also learn that the sexual aspect of love is limited; they know from experience that the best of all possible orgasms does not bring about fulfillment five minutes later. Some then come to see sex with a more balanced eye—as a form of play and pleasure but not as *the* basis for development in marriage. And then they may begin to build a more valid and more lasting foundation for a successful marriage.

In this search for ways to achieve marital growth, some couples are turning to celibacy in order to be entirely free of the sexual focus. In turning their sexual freedom around 180 degrees to celibacy, they are seeking to establish an entirely different basis for marital happiness and love. Celibacy can enable them to explore more deeply what they have together without the domination of sex. In this way, celibacy is a means to bring out and acknowledge the hidden values of marital love.

CELIBACY IN MARRIAGE

Celibacy or continence is presumed healthy for priests and nuns, the unmarried, children, the elderly, those institutionalized, and members of the armed forces away from home, but it is considered unhealthy for married adults.

—JOEL FORT, M.D.

It does not follow that the celibate and the couple are, as people think, in an opposite sexual situation. For both, continence is necessary. For the celibate, it is not only a matter of doing nothing. It is a matter of knowing oneself to be fully a man or fully a woman having social relations with men and women. Chastity alone makes this possible by triumping over the temptation to limit one's concept of sex to sexual desire. . . . Man and woman form a couple. This is the conjugal love of which the genital aspect is only one necessary consequence.

—PAUL CHAUCARD

> Without chastity, it is impossible to maintain the
> dignity of sexual love.
>
> —HAVELOCK ELLIS

Perhaps Mary and Joseph were the most well-known celibate couple. If they were the first, George Bernard Shaw and Charlotte Payne-Townsend could be the next best-known. They even signed a contract to maintain celibacy throughout their marriage.

But you generally don't hear too much about celibate marriage. (In fact, "celibate" from *caelebs* meant "single.") The idea that celibacy can be practiced during marriage may be as strange a concept to some people as the idea that priests can marry is to others. The traditional separation between celibacy and marriage is as strong as the traditional separation between sexuality and the priesthood. This would not be of much concern except for the unfortunate conclusion that spiritual development is associated with celibacy and not with sexuality. So marriage, in its commitment to procreation, has been aligned with sexual-nonspiritual life and the possibility of spiritual development is "saved" for single people—and generally only those committed to a religious vocation.*

Whereas love has been granted a spiritual component throughout history, especially by the poets, musicians, and artists, marriage has tended to be viewed as a more mundane affair, filled with worldly responsibilities and not really offering a good opportunity for higher development. And throughout most of history, marriage was based on economic and social considerations and had little to do with romantic love relationships, which were considered to be

---

*One noteworthy opponent of this predominant view was Henry David Thoreau, who considered marriage only worthwhile in the most rarefied form of spiritual love. He wrote: "If it is the result of a pure love, there can be nothing sensual in marriage. Chastity is something positive, not negative. It is the virtue of the married especially. All lusts or base pleasures must give way to loftier delights."

separate from marriage. Love and romance, as the basis for forming a marriage, were to come much later and in some cultures have never been the purpose of marriage.

Love and Marriage: A Recent Event

Love and aversion both wear off in matrimony, so
that it is better to begin with a little aversion.
—MRS. MALAPROP

Our concept that "love and marriage go together like a horse and carriage" is a relatively modern concept and is primarily a Western innovation dating from the time of the French Revolution. As odd as it may seem to us now, the idea that marriage could be the outcome of romantic love did not arise in our own culture until less than a hundred years ago. Marriage as a social merger based on economics, social status, family needs, and the like has always taken precedence over romantic love as the prime reason for marriage, even when great pain was inflicted on countless romantic lovers as the result of forced separation.

So love-and-romance marriage, although a testimony to the openness of a society willing to support a nonmaterial basis for a traditionally social enterprise, has not always been regarded as the most successful formula for marital life.

Bertrand Russell, like many before him, saw marriage as a means to fulfill a social purpose based on "affection and realism," not on romantic response. Fifty years ago he noted: "In America, where the romantic view of marriage has been taken more seriously than anywhere else, and where law and custom alike are based upon the dreams of spinsters, the result has been an extreme prevalence of divorce and an extreme rarity of happy marriages."[2]

In our society, we tend to consider romantic love a more valid or at least a more civilized reason to be married than if the marriage is "arranged." Yet such a basis for marriage does not seem to bring about lasting enjoyment or commitment. As Haich notes, "We are driven to the somewhat curious conclusion that the more civilized people become, the less capable they seem of lifelong happiness with one partner."

It may be that romantic love is not offering married couples a strong enough basis for a continuing commitment of growth in marriage primarily because the spiritual content of love has been kept separate from the usual commitments of marriage.

Today, when marriage is supposed to be based on a contract of love, it is still not understood as a channel for spiritual growth, and the historic distinction (in the West) between sexuality and spirituality still reinforces a primarily nonspiritual attitude toward marriage. But if the spiritual dimensions of love were added to the social-material enterprise of marriage, then hopefully all aspects could flourish.

Celibacy can be regarded as a way to "spiritualize" sexuality in order to refine the experience of love further. When a couple feels deeply connected and chooses not to express the love sexually, other ways to express those feelings start to emerge. When people are used to expressing love in the same way over and over, its expression is eventually reduced to just one channel, to one habit. But if love is redirected away from its usual channel, it finds new and perhaps more direct channels to flow in.

In this way, celibacy provides married couples with more choices of expression—a kind of limitless market of possible connections. It may be like "courting" all over again, but without the fear of rejection or the limitations of future goals. If a husband or wife brings flowers to his or her spouse as a first step or prelude to a great night of sexual love, the meaning of the flowers becomes lost in the chain of events that follow. But flowers in times of celibacy are a thing-in-themselves—perhaps the whole expression of love for that day—not simply an offering to insure the future.

All the ordinary activities of a shared life may in fact take on new meaning and have greater value for a celibate couple. Without the old pathways of sexual exchange to rely on, love seeks and finds other levels of exchange. And these may, in turn, provide increasingly more unbounded, more refined, more fulfilling experiences in the marriage.

Celibacy Is Never Having to Say "You're Boring"

When certain associations stemming from the past personal histories of individuals have linked sexual activity with restrictive qualities such as dominance, control, bribery, "scoring," and even more negative characteristics such as anger, resentment, jealousy, possessiveness, and emotional separation from sex, sexual love is at its least expressive level of fulfillment and may cause only unhappiness for a couple. To break the unfortunate patterns of association which have set in, celibacy can be used to enable love to be re-experienced at a purer, less complicated level of feeling.

Celibacy can give the couple the chance both to re-establish presexual communication of tender feelings and to open new channels of expression free from restrictive associative behavior. It can be a time for the renewal of old feelings that occurred before sexual habits set in, and it can be a time to discover other modalities of loving. It can re-create and create the unbounded qualities of romance—the intensity, energy, sweetness, simplicity, and careful attention of two people falling in love.

An interesting phenomenon that happens in marriage is the uniting of the physical lives of the two. Happily married couples are often thought to look alike after a number of years—even if they started out looking very different from each other—as if they had exchanged some features and grown together physically. One view of why this happens is the idea that the nervous systems of the two actually begin to interconnect through an exchange of energy. The exchange begins initially on the level of sexual expression and continues to grow in more subtle and more powerful ways over time.

If sexual interests start to fall away during marriage, it

may be because the physical union of the couple is already operating in a continuous shared flow of energy in all marital activity. Some couples feel a continual outpouring and intaking of love and energy, particularly when a profound basis of trust and devotion has founded the kind of open receptivity needed for such an exchange. So the uniting of the physical ties that one yearns for in sexual union is already occurring and the sexual activity may therefore be experienced as unnecessary or even undesirable—as a breaking of the flow, providing a less refined expression of an experience that is happening at more delicate levels of the physical nervous system and other body functioning. This more subtle exchange is experienced in feeling and thought—"being on the same thought wave"—in exchange of looks, hugs, and the energy felt sharing the same environment, the outer environment reflecting the inner.

This growth from expressed sexual union to a perhaps more intimate physical union is a common experience of marriage but one our society tends to overlook in the face of the popular, if misguided, desire to hold on to the success of concrete sexual activity as the most significant expression of physical marital union. But when a couple has the chance to enjoy what they share at these deeper levels, without feeling concern about keeping old sexual habits maintained as *the* proper procedure of union, they may realize that they are experiencing a fuller range of love, a richer emotional and spiritual bonding together. This does not mean that sexual expression is forever eliminated: it merely allows what may be a natural kind of evolution to occur, and the sexual may continue to be enjoyed but in a less important role in the achievement of the physical aspect of marital union.

This phenomenon is most clearly understood if we consider, as we will in the following chapter, how sexual energy is transformed spontaneously into other kinds of energy in human development: how all the energy may be really the same but expressed in different ways according to the level of consciousness of the individual expressing it at any given time in his or her life.

Experiences of Marital Celibacy

One aspect of celibacy in marriage that can occur is nonmutual celibacy, where one partner becomes celibate but the other doesn't. Just as sexual interest in marriage can grow more intense in one partner than the other, so can the desire to be celibate. But it is incumbent upon the partner who is undergoing the change in desire or behavior to be responsive to the feelings of the other.

If one partner wants to become more sexually active, it is usually because he or she feels unfulfilled sexually, which sometimes can be a focus for a more generalized lack of fulfillment. This situation is not uncommon in marriage; solutions dealing with it are suggested in numerous books on sexual relations. But if one partner wants to become celibate (and this could also be a common experience), there may be some confusion as to how to evaluate that desire in the context of marriage.

Essentially, it must be determined if the desire is due to a negative or a positive motive. In marriage, if one withholds sexual activity for negative reasons—to punish, control, or withdraw love—it is obviously not celibate behavior that can benefit a marriage. Going "on strike" against sex as the result of some argument or some temporary negativity is also not a useful assumption of celibacy. How then does a couple know if the desire to be celibate is positive?

Celibacy in marriage does not come about all of a sudden. If it does, it is suspect.

The growth toward celibacy, if it occurs at all in marriage, has been found to be a natural progression over time, not an immediate decision.

This point cannot be too greatly emphasized. Celibacy in marriage should only be practiced if it is comfortable for both partners and has been arrived at in a natural way. If one partner wants to be celibate but the other does not, the situation could create a major difficulty that can only be worked out in favor of the most sincere desire of both partners to further the growth of their love and commitment. If one can convince the other that a fuller experience of love lies ahead, the decision to be sexual or celibate will be based on that goal of increased happiness. Celibacy or sexual activity chosen *in the service of love* is the context in which a couple makes its decision.

How Long to Be Celibate?

Another consideration of marital celibacy is the issue of time. It doesn't matter how long a couple continues to be celibate if the situation remains progressive and comfortable. Some couples are celibate for years—either in the later years of marriage, when sex no longer holds its former fascination yet love continues to grow—or sometimes in the early years, when a couple may be seeking to establish the most intimate pathways for their love to flow beyond the limits of sexual expression. Other couples are celibate for a week or two—which may offer the chance for sexual activity to rest, to be renewed at a deeper level of settledness and for patterns of exchange to be restructured beyond the insistence of habit.

By the same token, a couple would want to avoid getting into a habit of being celibate if the enjoyment of the growth of love had ceased. If celibacy occurred as the result of an overall lack of desire to be together or as a kind of withdrawal of mutual love and support, then it may be time to re-examine the motives for the lack of sexual activity. So the practice of marital celibacy and the length of time a couple might wish to maintain it will be dependent upon the kind of growth experiences they are sharing and the fulfillment it brings to the marriage.

The commitment of marriage is to the other's growth in life as well as to one's own. These are the bonds of marriages and love. Bertrand Russell wrote: "Love must feel the ego of the beloved person as important as one's own ego, and must realize the other's wishes and desires as though they were one's own.''

Once a couple is united in commitment to each other on the basis not of need but the desire for the other's personal growth to fulfillment, marriage becomes an ideal avenue for social and spiritual development and accomplishment. The two unite, forming a base of strength and a broad channel of energy to give to humanity.

From this commitment marriage becomes a medium of service—to each partner from the other and from both partners to the society and the world. Growth in devotion, growth in surrender, and growth in outflowing love from an increasingly fuller heart are the signs of progress.

To maintain and advance the growth and flow of love in this ideal state of marital union, there have been couples in both past and present who have found that being celibate from time to time—even for a long period of time—provides certain profound benefits. Some decide to be celibate to achieve the benefits of a fuller love; others become celibate and then realize the benefits they have been experiencing through the growth of love. In either situation it is the expansion of love which is desired and created.

THREE CELIBATE COUPLES

The perspective of celibate marriage can perhaps best be described by those who practice it. What follows are interviews with three married couples who are currently celibate, with some additional history to present the sequence of experiences that led to marital celibacy.

Tom and Diane
Both are twenty-eight—Tom is a medical student and Diane runs her own greeting-card business. Tom and Diane have been celibate for three and a half years, married for five years, and have lived together on and off for over ten years.

They are an energetic, bright, humorous, and lovable couple who have a great number of friends and who maintain close ties with their families.

DIANE'S STORY. Diane grew up in a successful farming community in Illinois, the second of six children. Her father is a business consultant and her mother is in charge of the family's farm operations. Diane is a very warm and attractive woman. She describes her family as always very physically affectionate and open about sexual matters—where talk about sex was commonplace. She says that she has always been "a physical person" and that sex was "never a big deal for her"—she was comfortable with her sexuality from the beginning. During high school, she had several boyfriends and experienced a lot of physical relating. She would have slept with her boyfriend in her senior year but "there was never a really good opportunity."

In 1968, Diane went to college and met Tom at a picnic in the first week of her freshman year. "On the surface," she remembers, "he was cool and tough, but I sensed his soft core. He seemed much more sophisticated than he really was." According to Diane, it was purely accidental that she was still a virgin when she met Tom, but he saw it as a symbol of the purity of her nature. "He didn't want to 'corrupt' me, but I knew we were going to be together sexually. In one sense, we slept together because it would have been too big a deal if we didn't."

They started living together despite some doubts, especially on Tom's part. They both acknowledged that they would be married one day, but that a lot of growth would have taken place. Tom would say "I know I'm going to marry you, but I just don't want to be with you right now." In the summers they would be apart. Diane would return to the family farm and spend time with the hometown boys. Her main attraction to these other men was physical, she remembers. She had five or six of these physical affairs but would always long for the deeper connection she had with

Tom. Sex with Tom was a nice, but not essential, part of the relationship. Diane realized even then that perhaps the sexual aspects were becoming to some extent minimized.

TOM'S STORY.   Tom spent his first twelve years in the Midwest, and then his family moved to Washington. His father is a doctor and his mother a teacher. He has one younger sister. Tom recalls his early sexual life as "normal" but feels that perhaps he was "more sexually oriented than most kids" he knew.

In the eighth grade, Tom experienced his first orgasm with a girl and "connected sex and woman for the first time." At his school, he became part of a fast crowd. He learned that "sex is what you should always want if you're a real boy. In this pursuit, I was inevitably stopped in my quest by girls who knew how to defend themselves." By the eleventh grade, Tom had "done" it but had also by this time managed to separate sex and feelings "as the result of internalizing experiences of rejection." His rules became: (1) "Get it on" and (2) "Don't get hurt." "I knew I wanted sex," he recalls, "but I definitely protected myself from love." He convinced his girlfriends that they couldn't love him because he wouldn't love them. He slept with whomever he could—perhaps fifteen to twenty girls. He felt he had an image to uphold. "It would have been another moral plane for me at that time to have seen a girl and not have wanted to sleep with her."

Tom remembers having fun but being unable to let himself go. He was quite emotionally inhibited; his sexuality was very localized and never seemed to "soar." He was still eager to prove himself, but by the time he started college, he realized that he needed a more mature relationship based on feeling, even though "I still hadn't outgrown my Don Juanism."

When he met Diane at the beginning of his freshman year, her innocence dazzled him. "I didn't want to abuse her like I felt I had abused all the girls in high school. I knew *here* was a girl I could really love who could help me to love her and the relationship will go beyond sex finally." They became "best friends"—a friendship of intimacy. They also slept together "primarily to release the sexual tension" between them, but it was difficult for Tom to reconcile sex and love and commitment. "I was nowhere near integrated enough to be with her, yet I knew I wanted to marry her. I told her everything I could think of to turn her away from me, including tales about the other girls I slept with. I did a lot of sexual fantasizing *except* about Diane.

"In some way, sex for me was associated with violence, with animalism, with a lesser part of my true self. I couldn't really express my best nature in it. Diane's more uninhibited sexuality was hard for me to deal with. I wanted her to reach into me and pull me out of myself. But when she was very physical, she would be lost from me in her orgasm, emotionally apart, and I would feel isolated. I'd be withdrawn inside myself, and she'd be having these ecstatic experiences."

What developed was that when Tom and Diane were not getting along, when they were not touching each other emotionally, they would reunite sexually: the physical would bring them together. But when they were open emotionally, then "sex was not as enjoyable." "I wanted us to be parallel in our sharing and not be overwhelmed by sex. Diane thought I wasn't attracted to her, but I longed so much for her on a deeper level that I couldn't express it sexually. It wasn't enough." They developed a more passive approach to sexuality which was less "violent, softer, and seemed more in tune with our sharing of feelings."

A year before the marriage, Tom underwent a lot of changes. He grew from feeling contained, where the thought of a commitment to Diane "felt like being trapped" to feeling more and more open, free—a release of blocked feelings. At the end of his senior year, he reconciled his behavior by accepting himself as a man who preferred to relate to his lover on other than a sexual basis. In this resolution, he felt a strengthening in his commitment to the marriage.

Diane and Tom were married after living together solidly for a year during which time they had sex together maybe twice a month. Once married, Diane was still interested in sex, but Tom had really begun to want to be celibate. "She thought I was really neurotic—maybe I was—but I felt I had to keep our relationship in a deeper state than the sexual. I wanted us to be celibate so I could relate to her without any of my trips, in a full way without the challenging nature of the sexual encounter."

Diane recalls that she eventually began to understand the extent of Tom's desires to be more integrated in his feelings. He in turn, she says, grew more loving, more expressive and more intimate in the sharing of his feelings with her, and she eventually overcame her fears that he wasn't really attracted to her. "The real attraction was very powerful." By the second year of marriage, they both agreed to be celibate on a semipermanent basis, but with the idea that they would see what would happen in the growth of their feelings.

Several years later, Tom and Diane are still celibate and able to look over the results.

Some Questions and Answers

What do you get out of being celibate?

DIANE: Now, being together is like making love all the time. That may sound absurd to other couples, but celibacy seems to keep our hearts open to each other. Sort of the way it feels when you first fall in love. . . . It's similar to this article I read which said that people who got along best as friends had the least amount of sex in their relationships. That the negativity between people seemed to increase the desirability of sex.

When did you decide to be celibate?

TOM: We were already pretty much celibate, when we decided to be celibate!

Do you have any sort of physical relationship?

DIANE: We always play together. And we sleep together. We cuddle, we kiss and hug a lot. It's very spontaneous, but we don't get aroused to the point of intense sexuality.

TOM: It's something of the comfortableness that comes after sex—with the tension gone and just pure enjoyment. Maybe you could call it "hindplay." I never used to enjoy touching after sex. It would feel too personal, too real—without a goal, like the goal of foreplay.

Are you sexually attracted to people outside the marriage?

TOM: When I see attractive women, it's not exactly nothing—I look, but it's an appreciation—almost an aesthetic experience. I once heard a guy say almost that exact same thing about his reaction to beautiful women and at the time, I thought it was bull, but now I know what he meant. The physical desire just doesn't take you over in that overwhelming way, and you can really fully experience the woman's beauty without wanting to "have" her.

DIANE: The thought of sex with anyone other than Tom doesn't appeal to me at all right now. And with Tom, it's grown into something else.

How do you experience your celibacy?

DIANE: It's a pure thing. We feel good in it—in its purity. The reward is the "high" we feel together.

Besides that feeling, what keeps you both being celibate?

TOM: Until I feel that I'm better integrated about sex on an emotional level, I feel more comfortable, more in tune with myself being celibate. The supreme test for me would be if I could have sex and enjoy it and it equaled how I feel emotionally. It still feels less than full to me, and it doesn't express what I feel for Diane.
DIANE: At this point, it's a lot easier for me to not have sex than to pass up an ice-cream cone. Being in the habit of not having sex makes it a lot easier, and I'm very much in love with Tom in this way.

How about having children?

TOM: We'll probably have children in a few years. It will be an act of love to have a child—something divine.

Do your parents know you are celibate?

DIANE: My mother knows. At first she thought I was unhappy because we were celibate, but now she sees the positive strengths of our marriage, and she thinks it's good.
TOM: My parents would think it was the end of the world if they knew.

Does celibacy have a purpose for you?

DIANE: Celibacy kind of lets us be spiritual together. When we have sex again, we don't want it to be a downer but an act of worship. We see sex as being transformed into a different kind of experience through celibacy—making our love stronger within each of us and then into each other.

Peter and Anne

Peter and Anne have been married for eleven years and have been celibate for two years. They have two sons—the oldest (age sixteen) is from Anne's first marriage and the other was born nine years ago. Peter is a contractor and Anne is an interior designer. They live in Philadelphia, where they have a successful business redoing old houses and apartments. They are a witty, urbane couple—easy to be around—who seem to have a deep understanding between them and a mutual high regard. They say that they've "weathered the storms of marriage" and feel they have the right to decide the rules for themselves "but not for others."

ANNE'S STORY. Anne is a tall, strong, lively forty-year-old woman who grew up in Cincinnati in what she calls a "strict WASP home." Her father was a salesman and her mother raised the three girls, of whom Anne was the eldest.

Anne recalls very rare discussions about sex with her parents; she learned from her peers. Her first "celibate love affair" occurred when she was thirteen. "He came up to my shoulders. It was definitely True Love." During her high school years, Anne became part of a group "who turned out to be the fastest girls in the school." She became what she calls "a social deviant," at least in the eyes of her family. She began drinking and bringing her various drinking companions home with her. She wrecked her father's car and generally "enjoyed doing what I wasn't supposed to do." She had a few sexual experiences starting in her junior year, "but I didn't know what I was doing and I knew absolutely nothing about birth control." All in all, she says, "I think I got over that whole uptight upbringing I had in one wild year. But sex was really not much more than a lot of dirty jokes to me."

Once at college, Anne's behavior and outlook changed. She settled into her school activities gratefully. During her second year, she met Victor, her first husband-to-be. He was "handsome and romantic—right out of a picture book." They started going together and Anne observes that her "sex education really began with Victor at this time." They married when they graduated; Anne was twenty-two.

The romance carried Anne through several years of a rocky marriage and the realization that Victor was very unstable. Their time together was "a constant challenge." "We really lived in a fantasy. We prolonged the romance through a number of emotional tricks but we never really dealt with each other as people. After our son was born, I was forced to take a good look at what we were doing. I was definitely ready for a more honest and mature relationship, and it sent Victor right out the door. He wasn't prepared to make a commitment to a wife and family."

Alone with a year-old child, Anne started working out of her home. In time, she built up a successful decorator business in her community. She was happy and fulfilled at one level, "but I was always looking for someone to be with after the work day was finished, and I would feel a wave of loneliness. I never really longed for sex; I longed for someone to look at, talk to, and touch."

When Anne met Peter, "I knew he was someone extraordinary—a man who could see me as a person *and* who really could appreciate my womanliness. He wanted that part of me—the tenderness, gentleness, and passion—the part I didn't get to use in my business. Things between us grew slowly; I never felt rushed or that I had to prove myself quickly to him before he found someone else."

"We were together for almost two years before a real bond was established.During that time, Peter and my son also became close in a gradual way. Sex was part of our courtship and we enjoyed it—but it too was not frantic or rushed. We were growing together on so many levels; sex was just one combination among many. And never the most important."

PETER'S STORY. Peter, forty-seven, is a big, bearded man—quiet, warm and attractive. He was raised in New York, an only child, by his maternal grandparents after his parents were divorced. His mother spent most of his growing-up years on the stage and although there were a lot of visits, he couldn't really depend on her for his daily routines. He describes himself in those days as a child who became quite self-sufficient on the surface—"a tough loner" who really yearned for more attention.

As a result, Peter's first experiences of dating in high school were "very intense." He was torn between fear of being rejected and "wanting the experience of love so badly that I could barely stand it." He adds: "Sex was a definite thrill for me because it involved so much intimate contact and fulfillment of my fantasy life, but it was also terrifying to someone so needy. I was very easily won!" But like most high school boys, Peter was required to be "cool," to make it seem as if only the sex part mattered, when in fact he was most attracted to the emotional aspects of being with girls.

While at college in the East, Peter continued to be more or less a loner until he became involved with one woman in a relationship that lasted three years. They were comfortable together, sexually happy, and although Peter wasn't ready to be married, he felt relieved and thankful to have a close relationship. "She reassured me in a very basic way that I was a worthy partner and someone who deserved to be loved."

After they broke up (because Peter was unwilling to marry at the time), Peter returned to his former uninvolved status but felt good about it. Most of his time and energy were spent developing his business—an activity he thoroughly enjoyed. He had only one other relationship prior to Anne. "I had my share of one-nighters, but they weren't very rewarding. Sex for me really required a commitment to someone, and I was just too engrossed in myself and my work to be open to anyone. It was too distracting."

When Peter and Anne met, Peter was thirty-four and "pretty much the perennial bachelor." They were introduced by mutual friends, partly for business reasons. Peter describes his response to Anne: "We were united in some way almost from the moment we met. I sensed that Anne was a very unique, complete person. We didn't need each other but we wanted to spend more and more time together. We did this under the pretext of business. Working together provided a way for me to make a commitment to her."

Peter saw in Anne "a reason for me to have a life companion," and when he decided to marry her and become father to her son (and later their own second son), "it was the best decision I ever made."

Some Questions and Answers

Why did you stop having sex?

PETER: To be honest, and with all due respect to couples who will enjoy it forever, sex became fairly routine for us and not more rewarding than making love without sex. *Anne* never became boring to me but orgasms did. Not totally boring *during* sex, but I would feel often wiped out afterwards and think, "This is not where I want to put my energies, and it does not make me feel closer to Anne."

ANNE: To me, sex feels like a way to get to know someone. It's what attracts you at first but once you know them, sex is no longer so necessary. At least this has been my experience. I had a lot of sex in my first marriage and kept trying to get close to my husband and never did. With Peter, we have very little actual sex and a huge amount of closeness and love. Maybe we just are people who don't need a lot of sex together.

Why did you become celibate two years ago—at that point in your marriage?

PETER: Well, we say that's when we started being celibate but actually our sexual activity has slowly waned over the years. It just seemed more honest to say we were celibate when we finally acknowledged it two years ago. By admitting our status to each other, we avoided falling into the trap of secretly thinking something was wrong with us. *We* knew it was okay for us to be together and in love and not have sex, but we didn't know anyone who we were sure would agree. So it was a private affirmation of the value of our marriage without sex.

ANNE: I think I always knew we'd be celibate one day. Sex was good but it never had kept up with love. I actually looked forward to being celibate. When we knew we weren't going to have more children, sex became less significant somehow. I know that sounds positively Victorian, but that's how I felt. I am just as happy—I would say even more so—to be in Peter's arms or to hold him in mine.

Do you talk to your children about your being celibate and do you think that it has a different effect on them from when you were more sexual together?

ANNE: We never discussed our private sexual lives with them and we don't discuss our private celibate lives. What they know about sex is that it's something reserved for love, but that you certainly don't have to have sex to show someone you love them. They see us behave (usually) in quite loving ways towards each other, and I think they have a good feeling about their parents' marriage. And naturally, they know every detail of the sexual culture that they want to—we certainly don't refuse them information about sex. We just let them know it's not *our* number-one priority as adults.

How do you each integrate being celibate with your experience of being a man or a woman?

PETER: When I was younger, sex was on my mind a lot, but as I grow older, it seems to mean less and less to me. I know it is almost an obsession for American men. And maybe all men. Men together talk about sex constantly, especially in my business. Really, almost all the jokes in construction are sexual. And I'll talk like that on the job, too—it's the language you learn. But when I'm with Anne, and since we've been celibate, sex is much less of an issue to me. I think that being celibate has made me feel more integrated as a man. I experience myself as a multidimensional man—one with feelings, ideas, a creative mind, a humorous soul, etc. There is something strong to me about being celibate—being self-contained, powerful, virile. And yet still loving, warm, and tender.

ANNE: I see being celibate right now as being myself. In my early years, I never knew why people wanted to keep being virgins. I thought it was ridiculous, false, and prudish—that a real woman was a sexual woman. Now I have a much better appreciation for why a woman (or a man) might want to preserve her sexuality for a time when she knows that it represents how she really feels.

I have never really thought it was right to be defined as a woman by my sexuality. I am this person who happens to be a woman, and sex is somewhere on the list of things I can do, along with painting, dancing, cooking, etc. I do them all pretty well and none of them regularly.

Being celibate for me means being celibate *with* Peter. I don't know if I could have this with another man because our being celibate is based on the strength of our marriage.

Michael and Ginny

Michael and Ginny are in their fourth year of marriage and have been celibate for more than two years. They are a dynamic, vivacious couple who obviously enjoy each other deeply and are not afraid of showing their feelings. One does not have the impression at all of repressed sexuality smoldering under the surface, about to erupt. They seem altogether comfortable and happy.

GINNY'S STORY. Ginny is a very pretty thirty-year-old woman with a fluid, carefree, warm personality. She grew up in a wealthy Southern family who moved to a New York suburb when Ginny was nine. She was the oldest of three children. She says her family was always·very loving and very open with each other. Ginny was popular in high school and began "getting it on" at the age of fifteen. In the sophisticated high school she attended, this was typical behavior and "sex was what you did on a date." When she was sixteen, her father, an executive with the telephone company, was transferred to a Midwest city and Ginny was easily the most "hip" girl in her new high school class.

Ginny entered a "Big 10" university in 1967. She joined a sorority, but within two months "I became a freak." The drug era provided her with a lifestyle "which I absolutely loved." For the next three years, Ginny was The "most far-out" woman on the campus. "I went easily from politics into uninhibited hedonism." She slept with "uncountable" men, went to hundreds of parties, smoked a lot of pot and took acid. Still, she managed to graduate in 1971. Although she "definitely lived for the next party," Ginny had a serious side that kept her focused on her schoolwork.

As a "joyous hippie," Ginny enjoyed the freedom of "moment-to-moment" sex and the spontaneity of sleeping with everyone she wanted. When she met Michael in 1972, she was immediately taken with the strength of his personality and his radiance, "so unlike most of the men I had been with." He made it clear to her that he wasn't interested in a sexual thing, but that he was attracted to her in a profound way and wanted to pursue a friendship. His commitment to a "life of higher goals" had a deep appeal to her. She ended a relationship with one man she had been seeing "based on drugs" and became devoted to Michael.

MICHAEL'S STORY. Michael is thirty-four years old, an industrial engineer with a major national corporation. He is a very handsome man with movie-star good looks who glows with youth and health. Michael grew up in an upper-middle-class home in the suburbs of Detroit where he and Ginny now live. He has two older brothers and has always been close to his family.

Michael describes himself as a "long-time seeker." He had always had the thought of being a priest but, since his family wasn't Catholic, "it didn't seem like a very practical choice."

In the mid-1960s, Michael attended a Midwestern university where he discovered first radical politics, then drugs. He dropped out of the university twice and ended up moving to San Francisco in the famous summer of 1967. He pursued an interest in film, becoming a film distributor for a time, but then left for Europe. "I didn't find what I wanted there," so he returned again to the Bay Area, where he decided to become a farmer. He learned to farm and garden skillfully enough to become the caretaker on several large estates and loved the work. During this time he became interested in Eastern meditation as well. He eventually made his way back to the Midwest, where he completed his education and where he has continued to explore and develop his inner life along with becoming a very successful engineer.

Michael reports that he was not very sexually active in high school and tended to back away from sexual experiences that were available to him. He thinks that he "thought about sex far less" than the other boys in his class. He "didn't know much about girls," coming from an all-male family and felt he had a lot to learn about them in all areas, not just the sexual. He had one steady girlfriend, and he was happy with the nonsexual relationship.

In the spring of his freshman year at the university, he slept with a woman for the first time and enjoyed the experience. In the next year, he slept with about thirty more women and "although it was fun, I didn't like how I felt afterwards—sort of physically run-down and drained."

During his "drug days" in the Haight-Ashbury district

of San Francisco, he maintained a fairly active sex life, but his interest was not that strong. As he grew away from drugs and started turning to the life of a farmer, he began to explore Eastern mysticism, meditation, and spirituality. He read Yogananda's *Autobiography of a Yogi* and "although I didn't have any intellectual understanding of celibacy, I had a gut-level feeling that celibacy would be a great aid in spiritual development."

When Michael met Ginny in his home town in 1972, he had been celibate for a year and was quite committed to the experience.But he fell deeply in love with Ginny and had a strong intuition that "I was going to take care of that woman." Their love grew to a point where a commitment was called for, and Michael became "uneasy," wondering if his spiritual goals would be compatible with marriage. He remembers a friend saying "There's so little love in the world; don't restrict yours." He eventually became more comfortable in the relationship and felt more natural.

They had a long engagement of eight months, during which they were physical but not sexual together. "It was like courting." The tender, devotional aspect of their love grew, and they were married.

After they were married, Ginny and Michael made love sexually but felt that "sex wasn't as significant as it had been in our previous relationships with others." By about the third month, they were sexual only about once a week, feeling that "other aspects of our lives were more exciting to us." After about a year and a half, they decided to be celibate altogether and have been so for the past two and a half years.

Some Questions and Answers

Were you sexually attracted to each other when you met?

MICHAEL: Yes. Very much so, but the sexuality was more diffused than localized in its feeling—it felt more cosmic and universal than just specific and genital.

When you became less sexual after three months of marriage, did you think it was "normal?"

GINNY: Well, we thought it was normal because we talked about it, and it was what we wanted. Actually, I thought intellectually that we maybe *should* be having more sex, but it wasn't because I felt the desire for more sex, it just seemed more socially "correct" to be more sexual, but we would laugh about it.

MICHAEL: I had the feeling that sexual activity was not a necessity—I had heard of celibate marriages. After a time, the physiological need wasn't there, and it seemed more abnormal to have sex than not to.

Did you feel uncomfortable with your sexual desires once you decided to be celibate?

MICHAEL: Actually, it was the other way around. The desire seemed to decrease, and then I thought about celibacy. It was a great relief, as well as a great kind of freedom, to be free of sexual desire—it felt so comfortable.

Are you still at all physically attracted to each other?

GINNY: I've actually grown more physically attracted to Michael over the past three years, but I've learned to direct that physical energy in other ways. The desire automatically dissolves into waves of lovingness and the expansion of my heart towards him.

MICHAEL: I like the pleasure I derive from Ginny's "foxiness." She is a very physically beautiful woman, and I definitely prefer her to other women in a physical way. Our romance, like other romances, certainly has sexual attraction as one aspect. But the sexuality is just allowed to float into deeper feelings of love. We get much higher off it than when we were sexual.

Do you have any kind of physical relationship?

MICHAEL: Absolutely. We sleep together and hug and kiss and touch, but we don't pursue sex. Really, we have no physical boundaries at all. We feel deeply physically connected all the time and sex would more likely disrupt that flow than enhance it.
GINNY: What it has been like is a very long, delicate courtship and *very romantic*. It's ideal for a woman, you know—to have that tender side of a man always turned towards you.

Do your families know you are celibate?

GINNY: Definitely not. We would never discuss it with our parents. It's not a *cause* for us. At this point, although it is very natural for us, it's very private. Also, our parents want us to have children, and right now we're not sure we want to. But children and celibacy are two very different issues for us, and we don't want our families to confuse the two. Some of our close friends know and seem very intrigued by the idea of celibacy. We know two other couples who are celibate as well.

Do you recommend celibacy to couples?

MICHAEL: Obviously, we think it is a good idea for us because it has created such a smooth, loving relationship for us and, like we said, it feels very natural for us. But if it isn't natural, it would probably be a premature decision on the part of a couple. One thing to realize is that celibacy seems to arrive in marriage as something valuable. If a couple becomes less sexual together, it may be because their relationship requires more delicate kinds of love experiences than sexual activity. Then being celibate is a great way to explore that love. It seems to us like a step in evolution of love—from sex to celibacy.

Celibacy
and the Growth
of Consciousness

7   IT IS WELL KNOWN that one's body, thoughts and emotions all function together— interdependently. This is the fundamental outlook of Eastern health and medicine. But in the West there has been the tendency until recently to separate these functions. We go to one group of doctors for treatment of the body and another for treatment of the mind and emotions. With the advent of the holistic health movement, this piecemeal approach to human functioning is changing back to the treatment of the whole person, in keeping with the physiologists' view of integrated mind-body development. The study of human physiology is really the study of how the mind, emotions, and body all mutually support each other. This is also the study of human consciousness. How aware one is at any given moment—how alert, perceptive, intelligent, loving—that is, how "conscious"—is based on the functioning of one's physiology at the time.

Under most circumstances, whether we know it or not, growing increasingly more conscious is the better part of human development. In fact, the growth of consciousness is considered by many to be *the* essential purpose of life. Its ultimate goal is to bring about a state of permanent fulfillment in the individual.

Scientist-philosopher Julian Huxley had this to say

about the growth toward fulfillment: "Fulfillment seems to describe better than any other single word the positive side of human development and human evolution—the realization of inherent capacities by the individual and of new possibilities by the race; the satisfaction of needs, spiritual as well as material; the emergence of new qualities of experience to be enjoyed."[1]

In order to experience fulfillment, Huxley goes on to say, we need to develop lives in harmony with our "basic inner necessities" as much as in harmony with others, based on the evolutionary need to be as great as we can be, because, says Huxley, "No man ever achieves his real self until he is his best self."

In their original intent and most significant aspects, the rituals and structures of religion are designed to elicit the response of the growth of consciousness. This is the essential lesson in Judaism's Kabbalah, in Christ's teachings, in the mystic doctrines such as medieval alchemy, in the Eastern religions—in short, in practically all spiritual quests, past and present.

The growth of consciousness is also the primary message of modern psychology. As we look for ways to express love and creativity and ways to enhance mental and emotional experiences, what we are really seeking are ways to develop or unfold consciousness. It is this inner development of consciousness that leads to progressively more satisfying life experiences.

Celibacy and
the Evolution of Consciousness

> The history of human sexuality is the evolution of consciousness.
>
> —HERBERT RICHARDSON

Becoming celibate seems to occur spontaneously, like other natural events—in keeping with particular social, emotional, and spiritual needs and desires and with a corresponding minimizing of sexual urgency. This description of the celibate experience is at the heart of almost every discussion one has with people practicing celibacy.

If the possibility of celibacy is natural for some people at certain times, then there must be some aspect of human development which can enable this experience to come about naturally.

Celibacy outside religious life is very new to our society. Yet it seems to be emerging *now*, in an age of increasing emphasis on self-development, expansion of inner boundaries, wholeness of life, strengthening the society from within. The focus is more and more on new ways of relating to each other, new modes of interpersonal expression that take people beyond the ordinary experiences of daily routine. As personal goals change in line with the evolution of inner lives, sexuality is changing as well. As deserving this change, Dr. June Singer has written: "Evolutionary consciousness heralds the new age. . . . We are aware of how much we can control our sexuality and of the ramifications of all the ways in which we do control it." And, she continues: "The new era we are entering will require a shift from the exclusively personal viewpoint to one that includes the transpersonal, a shift from an egocentric position toward a universal orientation. . . . The new model of sexual consciousness will need to be inward-turning for . . . in order to be aware of oneself as a cosmic being, one needs to discover the nature of his own essence. . . ."2

One direction of that inward model is the turn toward becoming celibate. There is no doubt that such a shift is in keeping with the growth of consciousness. As Herbert Richardson has proposed, "Even to imagine the possibility that sexual desire can be renounced involves the presence of a new kind of consciousness."

In light of this new awareness, it is only natural that all aspects of sexuality be evaluated—not just *how* you are having sex or with whom but whether you really want to or not, whether having sex is in keeping at any given time with all other developments going on in your life.

There are those who believe that having sex is opposed to the growth of consciousness, at least sex with orgasm. Because when you have an orgasm, you actually lose consciousness for a moment. "Coming" is often followed by "coming to." The other times loss of consciousness occurs are during sleep, during illness (i.e., when you faint or are in a coma), or when you are overly intoxicated from some drug such as alcohol. Now, it is true that loss of consciousness during sex usually occurs for only seconds at most. But according to neurologist Richard Mayeux, reporting in the *New England Journal of Medicine*, it has recently been found that some people "experience a profound amnesia and disorientation for several hours after having sexual intercourse."

In the eleventh and twelfth centuries, notes Richardson, sex was considered sinful for just this reason: "Because it involved the temporary suspension of man's reason and voluntary freedom . . . at least in the moment of orgasm."

Yet today many practicing sex therapists advise people to *lose* consciousness during sex in order to have a "full" experience of it, in order to get them to stop thinking and analyzing during sex. As William Masters writes, "To a degree your own pleasure is dulled because you are not lost in the experience—you're observing. I am *not* saying that you experience no pleasure at all. I'm just saying that some of it is blocked. A level of perception is blocked."

So losing consciousness during lovemaking or being "lost" in the experience is said to be beneficially pleasurable for some people. But for those who are fully "there," who can maintain full alertness, observing is a very natural part of all experience—not something to avoid but something that increases enjoyment. And actually, one is really only fully appreciative of something if one is *not* overshadowed by it. By remaining within oneself, centered, aware, not lost in the experience, the chances are that the experience will be much more full, more clearly perceived, felt, understood, and enjoyed. This happens because as humans we have the unique capability of experiencing something and simultaneously being aware that we are experiencing it. So when we're having a good time, we *know* we're having a good time. But if we are doing something that *ought* to be pleasurable (from past experience) and isn't, we're aware that we're *not* having a good time. Such a situation occurs when there has been a change in consciousness and explains why desires, including sexual ones, change throughout one's life.

So the next question is: What is there in the development of consciousness that could lead a person to give up voluntarily that which affords so many of us such great pleasure?

THE NATURE OF PLEASURE

We can start by looking at the changing field of sexuality and consciousness from the view of physiology and ask, "Isn't sex always instinctively desirable in that it is always physically pleasurable?" The answer is yes and no. We are biologically structured to experience sex as pleasure, but we are also biologically structured to become celibate—to experience the growth from one kind of pleasure to other, perhaps more "pleasurable" pleasures.

According to Masters and Johnson, the basic physiological sexual responses remain the same regardless of the kind of activity used to achieve them. So we can conclude that although it's natural to be sexually responsive, the response itself doesn't really grow as one matures. And if other pleasures begin to replace the sexual response, the response can in fact diminish and give way to other kinds of more complex human pleasures such as emotions and ideas. As one kind of pleasure is replaced by a higher form of pleasure, the lower form is thus inhibited. As an example, women may experience feelings of contentment and deep joy during pregnancy and these feelings often serve as inhibitors of sexual desire.

Behavioral researcher H. J. Campbell presents a good summary of this possibility of physiological change. He defines pleasure as "simply the name we give to the subjective feeling we experience when our limbic areas are electrically active." He concludes that "the pursuit of pleasure is the *only* form of behavior" because when the pleasure areas are active, the impulses they generate reduce the electrical activity of the other behavioral areas.

The pleasure-seeking behavior of humans has a sexual component based on the male sex hormone found in both male and female that maintains the degree of pleasure-seeking. But at the same time, sexual functioning is the *sole* physiological process individuals do sacrifice for any number of reasons—whether for a higher goal or simply as a matter of convenience. "Everyone rejects sexual stimuli," observed Masters and Johnson, "when he feels that the circumstances are inappropriate." Or as Silvano and James Arieti contend, "Sexual pleasure may be the precursor of another type of pleasure that consists of spiritual and intangible qualities." This view of sexual development is based on the changes that can and do occur in one's physiological growth.

Campbell found that most long-term sexual relations were not rewarding if the partners continued to seek only autonomic sensory input during sex. Sexual sensory pleasure, he observed, is not generally progressive: it does not keep up with the growth one experiences in other areas. What Campbell suggests is that for sex to continue to be pleasurable, in keeping with other developments, people learn to derive sexual pleasure "not from sexual sensory input but from the descending impulses from higher regions." In other words, sex grows to be a mental pleasure more than a sensory pleasure and becomes infused in higher-level experiences. To explain this growth, Campbell outlines three stages of pleasure-seeking in humans:

1. Feeling-doing—an early stage where there is mostly sensory input and little higher level activity, such as thinking or intellect usage.

2. Thinking-doing—a stage where thought is turned into action which impacts on the environment and which includes most of life's activities. At the highest level of this stage would be creative expressions of thought, such as music and art.

3. Just thinking as a source of pleasure. This highest stage of human pleasure is found in mathematical and philosophical thought—where thought itself, without expressed activity, provides pleasure.

Campbell's physiological approach to the way we as humans learn and are physically prepared to experience pleasure is based on progressive and evolutionary growth from pure sensory experience to pure thought experience.

> Gradually, as brain maturation proceeds, the importance of sensory input declines. It never becomes irrelevant, but eventually the higher regions are sufficiently developed anatomically and informationally so that interchange between the thinking regions and the pleasure areas can be largely self-sustaining.[3]

Even animals have been found to want to progress beyond pure sensory reward. For example, rats that have been trained to use both a simple maze and a longer, more complicated one, when given a choice of a route to obtain food choose the more complicated maze.

But only humans derive pleasure from thought itself. And as Campbell maintains, "The clearest distinction we can make between the subhuman and human is that the human is able to evoke electrical activity in the limbic pleasure areas by processes occurring in the thinking region of the brain."

A scientist at work in the laboratory may not be regarded as someone having fun, but that's often exactly what's going on. Pleasure in one's work where one's mind is constantly stimulated and enlivened is an exclusively human source of pleasure and one that does not require any sensory input. Albert Einstein is one famous example of a person who experienced all his joy of discovery purely on the mental level, without any experience of the sensory world he was dealing with. In fact, his theoretical or "mental" discoveries were not even verified in the physical world until much later.

Higher emotional responses such as unconditional love are another nonsensory source of pleasure. And in fact, "the human brain can reach such a degree of sophistication" that one will lay down one's life for someone else or even for an idea. This kind of pleasure is exemplified in Wolman's Antigone Principle—a psychological model of altruism. Antigone is remembered for her willingness to die to uphold the dignity of her deceased brother, believing her sacrifice to be the most just and, to her, the most meaningful act possible. This principle is reiterated in the many human experiences where love draws a response greater than life itself: "This is my commandment: love one another, as I have loved you. A man can have no greater love than to lay down his life for friends" (John 15:12-13).

In light of the above, one can see that a person may *easily* give up the lower pleasures for the higher pleasures if his or her "pleasure response" is thus developed. What may seem like a great sacrifice from a lower-pleasure standpoint may feel very natural and right from a higher-pleasure standpoint.

This is one psychophysiological explanation for how we as humans advance. As sensory pleasure becomes more refined, higher states of consciousness are experienced. So as higher human pleasures come to replace lower ones, intellectual and emotional functions may minimize or inhibit sexual response.

Remembering that as one develops, sex becomes more complex and more mental, it is not surprising that this growth of consciousness could lead to another option—one of no sex or celibacy—if sex is replaced by other mental, emotional, or spiritual pleasures. Although in Western culture it is much less clear how celibacy fits into and advances psychosexual growth than in the East, this idea is nonetheless found in many of the developmental theories of Western psychology—where sexuality is understood as "one step along the way to developing the capacity to love."

The eminent philosopher Pierre Teilhard de Chardin describes the growth of human life as a series of steps in which a person integrates his self-love, his social life, and his orientation to God or spiritual life. Teilhard labels these steps of growth: affectionization, sensitization, and universalization. You begin the process by becoming "self-centered"—by becoming aware of yourself, and yourself in the context of sexual desires. Once comfortable with your own sexuality, you can become "socialized." According to Teilhard, it is only those of us who have really confronted the depths of sexuality, not only socially but physically as well, who feel comfortable as sexual beings, who are able to be fully socialized. And there are those who continue to grow beyond socialization to a "universalized" experience of sexuality—where tenderness and compassion are felt for all aspects of natural life. Thus, for some universalized people, celibacy is a kind of culmination of sexual maturity and development, enabling one to have the experience of universal love.

Teilhard's outlook is very similar to Abraham Maslow's. According to Maslow's research, the highest human need is "self-actualization" or the need to fulfill one's human potential. The higher needs are the more integrated, the more human responses which incorporate more of a person's capacities. In Maslow's hierarchy of needs, self-actualization comes after physiological and safety needs and after the needs for affection, achievement, and esteem. When we choose, Maslow says, we choose the higher need over the lower one, if we've been experiencing both.

In this "needs" progression, Maslow found that genital abstinence or celibacy is not in any way psychologically harmful in the most integrated, most self-actualized people functioning at the highest levels of human expression. What he found was that one's intellectual and emotional understanding and attitude toward celibacy is what makes it healthy or not. He found that self-actualized people preferred abstinence to sex without emotional or psychological commitment. (He also found that when they *are* sexual, they tend to enjoy it more intensely than others.)

If we compare Maslow's version of psychosexual development with Freud's, there is an interesting similarity. In both views, inhibition from one level of pleasure to the next is required for progress and growth. However, instead of one growing in a sense "freer" of sexual dominance, as in Maslow's needs progression, Freud held that as one progressed, one's sexuality became more inhibited and sublimated. Maslow's view is of love-based sexuality; Freud's view is sex-based love, with all energy as sublimated sexual energy expressed in various psychic ways. For Freud, sexuality was the prime mover of the human psyche and the only source of human energy. He proposed that all love and creativity—all the higher pleasures—are "aim-inhibited sexuality."

Many others such as Erich Fromm, Alfred Adler, and Carl Jung disputed this theory. They saw that if one carried Freud's analysis that all human emotion and activity is sublimated sexuality to its logical extreme, if sex were never inhibited there would be no tender love. They realized that there must be a *nonsexual* source for tenderness and love. For them, it was love, not sex, that formed the basis of their view of human behavior. Freud placed a heavy emphasis on sexual energy as the origin of behavior and was able to adapt his theory to all manifestations of human nature. But sometimes he had to bend a little to accommodate his observations. Such was the case with celibacy.

In Freudian terms, celibacy would be total sublimation of sexuality—a desexualization of drives into a generalized love for everyone. Because Freud theorized that sex was

the primary motivating force of human life, one would suspect, as June Singer has, that the Freudian view would
leave "hardly any place for a legitimate celibacy."

However, Freud was surprisingly open to the positive
results of celibacy. He observed that people can achieve
happiness by transcending sexuality for a higher experience
of love and took examples from the religious life. He cites
St. Francis of Assisi as the celibate who "went furthest in
thus exploiting love for the benefit of an inner feeling of
happiness." He wrote:

> These people make themselves independent of their object's
> acquiescence by transferring the main value from the fact of
> being loved to their own act of loving; they protect them-
> selves against loss of it by attaching their love not to individ-
> ual objects but all men equally, and they avoid the uncertain-
> ties and disappointments of genital love by turning away from
> its sexual aim and modifying the instinct into an impulse with
> an inhibited aim.[4]

In an article entitled "A Psychoanalyst's Case for
Celibacy," Dr. Jean Rosenbaum echoes this aspect of
Freud's evaluation in observing that celibacy, far from
creating neuroses through the sublimation of sexuality, can
serve to make manifest a great love and affection for all
humankind and the "desexualization of drives can be thus
turned into 'works of service,' benefiting society as greatly
as 'any creative life work.' " Perhaps then, in Freudian
ideology, the celibate is able to re-experience the pregenital
sexuality that Freud speaks of as "oceanic"—where love
and sex are not divided but begin together.

The Freudian view that all human expression and the
development of culture is really a sublimation of sexual
energy was an interesting assessment of the mechanics of
the development of consciousness. But Freud's concern for
this transformation was in its ability to establish the true
value of sexuality in all experience. The idea of a changing
sexual energy was valid, but Freud no doubt overestimated

the primacy of sexuality by placing it in the center of human development, instead of recognizing that, transformed, it became another form of energy.

Other Western psychologists—Jung in particular— broadened this understanding to include all psychic energy. Jung showed how human psychic energy could flow in a number of channels, including love, intellect, and creative and religious experiences. For him, the primary life force includes the sexual but is not based on it.

SEXUAL ENERGY: GAIN OR DRAIN?

> Conduct the water which is flowing into the sewer
> to the garden instead.
> —ST. AUGUSTINE

Throughout history, a universal idea has prevailed that sexual energy for nonprocreative purposes can either be "used up" in sexual activity or "contained" for upholding the development of the body and the mind. This sex energy was seen as the fuel for opening these channels of experience, not only in the East but in the alchemy of the Europeans during the sixteenth and seventeenth centuries. Moses was said to have requested soldier-husbands to refrain from marital sex to preserve their strength for battle. Ralph Waldo Emerson, when married, was also a believer in sexual abstinence for preserving his energy and wrote "I husband all my strength in this bachelor life I lead."

Even today there are people everywhere who maintain that physical orgasm has a draining effect on both mind and body that results in an overall energy loss in the system. To prevent this loss, many athletes, actors, musicians, and other performers forego sex before the game, the show, the concert. Basketball star Bill Walton estimates that about half the players he knows find it helpful to abstain before a game. The idea is that sexual energy is thus converted into a better performance.

Taken at its most superficial value, such a view may

appear repressive and "prerevolutionary." But if one explores it in more depth, this understanding of human sexual energy finds a surprising amount of support in a number of diverse places.

In his scholarly work on Eastern philosophy, Mircea Eliade wrote: "Modern science agrees with the ancient sages of the East . . . that what holds the universe together is the mysterious, non-individualized something we call 'energy.' "

R. Buckminster Fuller, the great synergistic thinker, helps us conceive of energy as a concept of wholes, not as discrete entities or parts. According to Fuller and others, an energy *system* or "whole" is the only valid way that energy has any functional meaning. Science presents this theory with the understanding that matter and energy are inseparable . . . and that the universe holds together based on their natural interconnectedness.

When this understanding of wholeness is applied to human sexuality, sexual energy is seen as a part of a larger, more universal energy. Sexuality becomes, as Jung and others saw, "only one way of expressing bodily and spiritually, that universal energy" that is incarnated in every human being, a universal energy that expresses itself through all of nature and that humans can express within their own lives however they choose. This is essentially the Eastern concept of the relationship between sexual and universal energy.

In the East, the expansion of consciousness and the transformation of sexual energy have been generally observed to be highly correlated events. Whether it is the expansion of consciousness that precedes any change in sexuality or the physiological results of the refinement of sexuality that bring about the expansion of consciousness is not really understood, but in either case the two are considered virtually inseparable.

In this view, sexual energy has two purposes: one is procreation and the other is its usefulness in the transformation of consciousness—from a near-animal state to a universal consciousness of God; from "unconscious" to "allconscious."

In order to accomplish this growth more quickly, the East has long promoted the use of traditional methods for raising the level of consciousness through techniques that serve to redirect energy within the body. Meditation and yoga practices help refine mental and physical energy, enabling the mind and body to function in a more efficient, coherent way. It is said that as physical energy is refined inwardly, it creates a more powerful base of functioning for all outward activities.

This transformation brings about some changes in physiology and some consequent changes in consciousness. To maintain this evolutionary process of accelerating the growth of consciousness, there are those who practice celibacy along with other technologies, believing it to aid in the transformation of energy. They contend that if one doesn't discharge sexual energy in orgasm, it becomes converted into other levels of energy. The idea is that the cells are revitalized by a high frequency of energy generated throughout the body, keeping one vibrant by maintaining a vitality of body and mind.

It is a form of self-actualization of the body that is integrated with mental powers. Whether achieved with the help of celibacy or not, this higher integration of mind-body functioning enables one to establish spirituality as a physical reality—the "magic" powers various people throughout history have attained were also said to be related to the physical manifestation of this high psychic energy.

Sexual desire is thus understood as one step in a series of energy transformations which bring about the growth of consciousness. In a person who is entirely "unconscious," says Elisabeth Haich, "the possibility of a transformation of energy does not even occur. . . . Therefore, he simply expends physical-sexual powers in a normal way, and not creative-spiritual ones." And if one tries to be celibate but is not physiologically ready for the experience, this is a form of repression of sexuality. The natural development only occurs because consciousness is based on a physiological readiness.

This formulation has been put forth to explain the mutual refinement of human consciousness and sexuality as well as certain aspects of human evolution. From this perspective, there are stages through which mankind evolves from an unconscious animal life to a dawning of consciousness, to an emotional life perhaps involving a spouse and family, to a desire for knowledge, to an inner awakening of creative expression, to a realization of universal and divine love and, finally, to a universal awareness manifested in a universal unity of consciousness.

Initially, society itself serves to help refine sexuality from its animal to its love nature, the process John Gagnon and William Simon refer to as socialization of sexuality. In most cultures, from primitive to advanced, young people are taught to postpone sexual fulfillment for some time. During this waiting time, sexual tension increases and when it does not get released, it gets transformed into a more complex social awareness which has been awakened by the desire.

The sexual urge thus gives way to a "higher," more lasting level of fulfillment—that of being in love. Richardson explains: "In persons who have attained a certain level of psychosexual integration, genital feeling is aroused only in conjunction with particular beloved persons, and the primary satisfaction gained from sexual intercourse is not orgasm but communion." From this channeling of energy into love comes a further development in the evolution of consciousness—the desire for creative expression.

Most experts seem to agree, no matter what the mechanics they favor, that sexual energy is somehow associated with creativity. But whether celibacy is a requirement for its favorable expression or not has been debated for centuries. According to one historian, in ancient times, the Muses were represented as virgins "to show the little disposition which the learned have for physical love."

Honoré de Balzac put it bluntly: "If you sleep with a woman, you leave your novel in her bed." As for Tolstoi: "Oh, if only I could be free from desire for three hours—how much more I could create." While for Thoreau, writing in *Walden*, chastity represented all that was best in man's creative development: "Chastity is the flowering of man; and what are called Genius, Heroism, Holiness and the like are but various fruits which succeed it."

Dr. Arthur Gould even proposed (obviously not in our era) that "all our great thinkers have affirmed the physical, mental and spiritual benefits to be derived from absolute chastity. . . ."

Today, Dr. Mary Calderone, a leading authority on sexuality, defines creativity as "simply the result of the evolution of the person to the point at which fulfillment of his highest potential becomes as easy for him as breathing." She goes on to explain how creative experiences may or may not require sexual tension at their base. But she reasons that as one grows in maturity and self-development, eroticism may well *decrease* and creativity increase: "As the individual matures (in the true as well as chronological sense), as his experiences of self and others deepen . . . his eroticism might appear to diminish, whether absolutely or relatively; but if the individual is free, the total in terms of creativity, should, I believe, increase."[5]

For a long time, Freud's theory identifying creativity as sublimated sexuality made creativity seem like a kind of second-class sexuality—valid, but not The Real Thing. But with the broader picture coming from Eastern sources as well as Jung, Maslow, and others, it is clear that the transformation of sexual energy into creative experience is a spontaneous consequence of human evolution and the development of consciousness and not a negative repression of an equally natural function—sex. Neither creativity nor sexuality is more "real"—both represent human nature at different levels of consciousness. And these levels can only be meaningfully experienced if they occur naturally.

AS CONSCIOUSNESS RISES

The refinement of consciousness and the refinement of sexual energy must be natural to be valid. Psychologists and others are careful to warn against trying to finesse stages of growth. They indicate that the physiological, psychological, and spiritual development of the individual has to be coherent and integrated. Consciousness demands balance in growth. That is why no one becomes celibate independent of other aspects of consciousness. Clearly, it's good to be as fully acquainted with sex as necessary, particularly if one harbors constant worries that something is being missed that would bring pleasure. If it is a sacrifice to give it up, why give it up? No self-respecting seeker renounces something for the sake of something less, only for the sake of something more.

However, there are some individuals for whom sex holds no fascination, presumably because they are experiencing levels of pleasure higher than the sexual. This comes about because apparently, as consciousness rises, one doesn't miss sex. There is a calmness, a clarity of understanding, certainly not an hysterical rejection. And as consciousness develops, giving up sexual activity is easy because other experiences are providing more enjoyment than sex. If there were no higher pleasures, there would be no reason to give up sex. Obviously, the great saints of the West and the great masters of the East would never have willingly renounced sexual pleasures if such pleasure could have brought them *lasting* fulfillment.

And it is at these higher levels of consciousness that the *desire* for sexual activity is said to "fall away like ripe fruit from a tree." Of course, sexual activity is still always available to such a person but is rarely chosen as a rewarding pleasure. So a natural desire for celibacy is said to occur.

And the conserved sexual energy is put to work in other ways, contributing, it is thought, to a strong and vital physiology that supports and maintains the permanent experience of higher levels of consciousness. Consequently, those who have achieved a permanent state of pleasure or fulfillment are said to radiate a kind of energy of love which is constant, unbounded, brilliant, and truly universal.

Attitudes
for Celibacy:
Letting go of sex

CELIBACY IN TODAY'S SOCIETY

Although not that many years have passed, ours is a very different time from when Thomas Mann wrote "The future is for the nations who are chaste" and from when Mary Baker Eddy observed that "Chastity is the cement of civilization and progress." But there is the possibility in our present-day society that we are in an optimal position to experiment with celibacy—to enjoy the measure of its freedom without the harm of sexual repression. And, in fact, we may need to try it.

As a society we've certainly learned that it's okay to be sexual. We've taken up the cause of sexuality and are avoiding repression eagerly. But what has been the result? For one thing, we're *still* obsessed by sex. At least we think its sex that we're always going to be longing for. And for another thing, because it's become so distorted, particularly in relation to all other social activites, it's not comfortably integrated into most people's lives.

If freedom from sexual tension had been a truly useful event in this society, leading to positive changes and at least the partial elimination of antisocial behavior associated with unfulfilled sexual needs, the issue of celibacy would probably never have come up. But actually, in the aftermath of the sexual liberation movements, when all that pent-up sexual tension would surely have been released, the results were just the opposite. In the "liberated" early 1970s, mental illness struck one out of four families, a murder was committed every seventy-two minutes, fifteen violent crimes were committed every hour. Without having to calculate exactly how much of this societal misfortune was due to sexual causes, we may speculate that perhaps too much attention to sex is at least as debilitating to a society as too little.

Celibacy may be one way to compensate for the overplay of sex. When sexual activity is overvalued and its "rest state" undervalued, the center of personal growth within the society may be off. Without knowledge of its unexpressed state, sexuality becomes diminished, unreplenished, and weakened. Celibacy allows sex to settle back into the fullness of its own nature, to experience its full potential and, subsequently, provides the opportunity for society to reinvest in other channels of human communication that we seem to need badly.

For while we've been concentrating on being sexual, we've neglected a lot of other paths of exchange. As Eugene Bianchi observed, "On the level of mind and decision in the public sphere, there is little or no intercourse between men and women. In this realm, our . . . society is as celibate as a Trappist monastery."

THE CELIBATE BALANCE

It is likely that if we were living in a way more "in tune" with the laws of nature and evolution, there would be no need to learn to be celibate because there would be no imbalance between sexual interest and human development, just as there is no overindulgence among the animals or in the simpler human societies. And this imbalance is not just a present-day phenomenon. As Bertrand Russell wrote in the earlier part of this century:

Sexual fatigue is a phenomenon introduced by civilization; it must be quite unknown among animals and very rare among uncivilized men. In a monogamic marriage it is unlikely to occur except in a very small degree, since the stimulus of novelty is required with most men to lead them to physiological excess. It is also unlikely to occur when women are free to refuse their favours, for, in that case, like female animals, they will demand courtship before each act of intercourse, and will not yield their favours until they feel that a man's passions are sufficiently stimulated. This purely instinctive feeling and behaviour have been rendered rare by civilization.[1]

We overindulge because we are constantly allowing ourselves to be aroused. So all techniques for celibacy pivot on giving the body a chance to rest, to get away from constant stimulation—to enable it to function in a different way.

Making Celibacy Conscious

> It makes no difference how we divert our attention from sexual desire, the main thing is that we divert it.
>
> —ELISABETH HAICH

There are really no instructions necessary for *becoming* celibate. All that is necessary is to *decide to be* celibate, for, as was pointed out in earlier chapters, celibacy is primarily a mental decision. We can choose to be celibate, as we can choose to be sexual—*if* we are consciously able to choose at all. To be celibate as opposed to frustrated or martyred, one must make a conscious choice for a good reason—on behalf of one's own personal fulfillment. And once we have chosen to be celibate for a time, the same principle applies to *remaining* celibate. To maintain celibacy, by far the best method, according to Haich and others is "never to lose hold of one's consciousness."

The Celibate Vow

A conscious choice sometimes takes the form of a vow. In a vow, you give up something good for something you think will be even better. A vow of celibacy can be religious in nature. Traditionally, in religion, celibacy is pledged as a vow of faith. For example, in the West, the priests, nuns, and monks of the Catholic church renounce their sexual activity in favor of a commitment to Christ through a vow of chastity, along with other specific vows.

Or the vow to be celibate can be secular. One vows to be celibate to develop a fuller spiritual life or a more powerful love relationship. In the East, the *bramacharya* vow of celibacy is also more than a decision to avoid sex. It is a commitment to personal growth based on the understanding that such a commitment is essential in order to experience higher states of consciousness and attain eventual permanent enlightenment. It is a dedication of the entire personality to a spiritual goal.

When we vow to love someone, either in marriage or another form of relationship, we envision that the situations in which we will love them "no matter what" will be smoothed over by the love we hold—that the growth of love through a commitment of devotion will be worth all the sacrifices along the way, that we will grow stronger and happier as we rise above all circumstances. Similarly, when one vows to be celibate in order to love more fully, there is the thought that the rewards of being celibate will exceed the sacrifice of sexual activity.

Thus, celibacy is not to be thought of as mere abstinence from sex, for that is what we all do most of the time anyway (at least most of us do). But it is more accurately understood as a conscious choice made on behalf of one's greater personal gain.

On the other hand, we certainly don't have to take a vow in order to be celibate. To maintain a celibate attitude does not require any vow at all. In fact, a vow could be decidedly wrong for some people, who would end up feeling bad if they broke it. So, for some, just keeping in mind that they're not going to have sex for a time is enough—just as for certain people, "not eating much" works a lot better than "going on a diet."

Whether or not it is an actual vow, once the mental decision to be celibate is made, it is the only real requirement for celibacy. It may have to be renewed from time to time, but it serves to set the activity of the body in a specific direction.

Mental Celibacy

The principle here is that thought controls activity. What we think determines what we do—what we have thought determines what we have done. So if you are going to be celibate, you have to instruct the mind to take a mental attitude of celibacy. And, in so doing, you would want to avoid the distraction of sexualized thought.

Masters and Johnson and others have recommended that when sex grows stale in a relationship, the couple pursue mental-fantasy exercises to generate more desire and interest in sex. We can assume that the opposite would hold true: in order to remain celibate (to be less sexually "desiring") you would *not* pursue active sexual fantasizing.

One method Elisabeth Haich recommends to gain mastery over sexuality is to "occupy the intellect with something else. . . ." She writes: "Two things cannot be in one and the same place at the same time. Therefore, we must expel all sexual thoughts from the intellect by replacing them with thoughts of a different kind. . . . We must learn to think about what it is we want to think about.[2]

This advice is not so simple to follow, however, especially if one doesn't have the kind of mind that can decide what it wants to think about. After all, if someone tells you not to think about elephants, what's the first thing you're thinking about? And if you're not *supposed* to think about sex, what else will the mind think about? So one must be relaxed about thinking; any sexual thought can come up, but you don't have to actively pursue it.

A modern priest, Joseph Wade, uses a simple approach. He counsels that, to maintain celibacy, one will do well to experience sexual feelings as "innocent, unreceived, and unwelcomed." He further advises to observe "a certain prudence" when dealing with the opposite sex, but he reminds us that a celibate "is not obliged to choose the more repressive and negative position in the manifestation of affection." In other words, you can be affectionate and loving even when celibate, as long as you don't encourage sexual desire. The key factor for a comfortable mental outlook on celibacy seems to be to keep it simple—and not to try and complicate the issue with behavioral analysis and rules. Celibacy is actually a lot less complicated than sexual activity—it involves doing nothing. So the best mental approach may be not to try at all—not to *try* to be sexual or *try* to be celibate. Just see what happens, keeping in mind what you want for yourself.

Physical Celibacy
To prevent specific arousal of localized sexuality in the body, sexually stimulating environments and physically arousing sensory experiences are naturally avoided. Sexual desire is said to be created through the senses. Impulses are sent from the brain, structuring the conditions for excitation. So celibacy is, of course, much easier to maintain when the senses are not bombarded by stimulants. Says Haich: "[There are] those people who do not leave their glands in peace, but rouse them with highly spiced food, stimulant drinks, erotic reading matter, films, and other such excitants. This only overtaxes the glands and weakens them prematurely."

In the East, advocates of celibacy have long recommended the avoidance of spicy foods such as garlic, onions, peppers, paprika, and the like. And, according to the *Kama Sutra,* a little alkali mixed into the food will render continence easier.

In the West, Dr. William A. Alcott, a noted champion of healthy living in the early nineteenth century, observed that

sexual desire could be substantially decreased by the elimination of liquor, smoking, coffee, tea, condiments, sugar,
lard, and spicy foods. "No man," he wrote, "has ever
become an adulterer, a fornicator, an idolater eating sim-
ples such as plain wheat, corn, rye, potatoes, rice, peas,
beans, turnips, apples." (One suspects that no man after
eating such a diet was ever even able to move from the
table!) Similarly, other sexual energy "savers" have out-
lined programs for celibate living that included going without tobacco and meat.

Foods generally regarded as aphrodisiacs would, of
course, be avoided. Seafood has been most highly praised
along these lines and would, therefore, be eaten with due
respect. Snails are said to contain a sugar found in male
seminal fluid and are thus thought to be highly "sexy."

Besides watching what one eats, advocates of celibacy
have also advised increased participation in active sports,
physical work, and specific exercises used to direct excess
energy and the flow of blood into all parts of the body. In
their book on hatha yoga, Michael Volin and Nancy Phelan
recommend several yoga postures for maintaining celibacy.
Among them are the eagle pose and the tree pose for males,
the frog pose for females, and the shoulder stand for both,
to help conduct the energy upward.

Volin and Phelan also note that in the East careful attention to the physical body is an important consideration in
the maintenance of celibacy. Thorough bowel evacuation
and bodily cleansing are said to help, along with some other
activities for the more Stoic, which include sleeping on a
hard board, the requisite cold showers, and squatting over a
basin of cool water while moving up and down slowly, im-
mersing the genitals.* It is also said that sleeping on the
back, which causes undue pressure from the bladder on the
areas in question, should be avoided.

*This, perhaps, could be modified by sticking one's feet in cold water
instead. Maimonides observed that when the feet become cold, sexual
arousal is diminished.

A Word on Masturbation

A surprisingly large number of people wonder if masturbation is "permitted" if one is celibate. Since being celibate (whether for a day, a week, a year, or a lifetime) means refraining from sexual activity and since many books on sex nowadays are giving masturbation the blue ribbon for most terrific orgasms, it is clear that if you want to indulge in celibacy, you don't masturbate.

It may seem that masturbation is a form of celibacy because you are generally alone when you do it, but since celibacy can be easily practiced by more than one person together, being alone is not a criterion for being celibate. Actually, masturbation is nothing if it is not sexual. It may be other things, too, but it is primarily a sexual activity, and since one wants to move away from being ruled by any behavior or any object of behavior, one may want to choose to avoid masturbation as one explores what it means to be celibate.

Notes from Tantric Technology

The Tantrics were and still are considered the world experts in sexual knowledge and techniques for channeling sexual energy. Although the Tantrics were not strictly celibate, Tantric techniques for the transformation of sexual energy recognize the tremendous power of human sexuality and make use of it in ways that are often contrary to Western experience.

One basis for their techniques (which are essentially male-oriented) is the importance they give to the value of semen for spiritual experience. Semen is considered to be the essential substance for male experience of higher consciousness and must therefore be conserved.

For the Tantric practitioner, the purpose of yoga practices is "to distill within the adept's body a golden liquid from which the elixir leading to longevity, immortality and mystical union could be formed." But being an adept is no simple matter. Volin and Phelan note that "As the celibate yogi conserves seminal energy through . . . transmutation, the Tantric also conserves it, even in the embrace of a woman, by hatha yoga techniques.''

The most celebrated of the techniques used to channel sexual energy is called *maithuna*. *Maithuna* is a ritualized procedure or extended technique for gaining control over one's sexuality generally during marriage. It is traditionally practiced during the first year of marriage. It involves the use of several techniques, ranging from meditation to the readsorption of the discharged semen.* It is not only a physical technology but a symbolic one as well, in that the rite is understood to represent a symbolic union of divinity within the physical union of the married couple. The purpose of *maithuna* is to move beyond physical gratification to a state of permanent blissful fulfillment in marriage.

The ritual is described by Mircea Eliade, who writes: "In preparation, the two people retreat to some secluded place, such as a forest. Here the couple will spend many months in each other's company." For four months, the man is the woman's servant, continually available to her emotionally so his devotion to her may grow. First he sleeps in the same room with her, then at her feet. For the next eight months the man and woman sleep in the same bed without sex, this time of celibacy bringing about a comfortableness and an 'autonomization' of physical sensuality. Here, the emphasis is on feeling, not genitality. Mastery of self-control is slowly learned as the husband becomes accustomed to the body of his bride. Once that has occurred, says Eliade, "He reaches a state of detachment where he neither desires her nor does he not desire her. He will have passed beyond the level of consciousness in which he demands personal or sensual gratification for its own sake."[3]

---

*In an advanced adept who has trained in the rite of *maithuna*, the ability to "return the semen" is said to be gained. The male is trained to be able to draw the seminal fluid back into his body while at the same time drawing in the fluids of his partner.

In *Island*, Aldous Huxley describes the ritual of *maith-una* as the regaining of the childhood paradise of unbounded sexuality—nongenital, unfocused, and unlimited in its joy: "What we're born with, what we experience all through infancy and childhood is a sexuality that isn't concentrated on the genitals; it's a sexuality diffused through the whole organism. That's the paradise we inherit. But the paradise gets lost as the child grows up. Maithuna is the organized attempt to regain that paradise."[4]

Huxley adds that this heightened control does not involve the repression of sexual feelings, but "its perfect integration with the voluntary capacities of man."

A Modern Outlook on Celibacy

There really aren't any basic rules for how to be celibate in Western culture, nor any definitive techniques. And there seems to be a much less sophisticated body of experiential knowledge in the West than in the East with regard to sexual functioning. According to sex researchers Gagnon and Simon, "work on increasing 'voluntary' control of sexual responses . . . is beginning only at the present moment."

Celibacy itself is currently considered a technique for enhancing sexual response. In fact, it is regarded as the best cure for impotence. It works because the body immediately starts to normalize its functioning and allows sexual response to develop comfortably from the "rest" state, when one's physiology is maximally prepared for activity. It is interesting to consider the possibility that impotence may be the body's way to take the rest it needs—physiologically imposed. Yet, impotence differs from celibacy because it is not an integrated state of functioning but rather indicates a breakdown in mind-body coordination—the mind commands and the body does not obey.

It is not surprising that celibacy revitalizes sexuality by giving the body the opportunity to rest. But, at the same time, it also revitalizes *all* parts of the body. It's a physical trade-off. Because the body functions as a system in which the workings of each part affect all others, celibacy changes not only sexual functioning but the entire physiology and total body functioning as well. By eliminating sex from daily experience, the body can become open to other physiological ways to expend the conserved energy, which include mental and emotional changes, experienced as greater vitality, more mental clarity and focusing ability, more refined perception, more profound feelings of love. Overall, says Haich, "My body calms down . . . yet it lives with much greater intensity and has much greater potency than the body of [one] who is still in the grip of sexuality."

Celibacy can help create a wholeness in mind-body functioning that contributes to a more equitable balance of physical, mental, and emotional functions. Keeping in mind that one is in a sense "donating" one's sexual energy to various other endeavors helps to promote a happy private experience of its value.

It is also useful to remind oneself that being celibate is an alternate way to love, even to make love. One can learn to touch nonpossessively, without a future goal—and to make love nonsexually, unmotivated by the need for sexual gratification. Being aware of one's sexuality and thinking about it as a passive state rather than an active one helps place the emphasis on a generalized feeling of love and well-being rather than on a localized response.

And, finally, it is clear that although one can decide to be celibate, a certain degree of consciousness must be present both to make that choice and to maintain it. No methods for celibacy are more important than this. And if one wants to, one can easily find a useful mental technique for developing consciousness with the accompanying benefits for body and mind.

What follows is a way to think about some of the advantages and possible situations which may arise from being celibate today.

HOW TO BE CELIBATE:
TAKING A VACATION FROM SEX

• It's not a diet or an exercise. It's a vacation from sex. So think of it as a vacation.

• During a vacation, you can expect to feel more rested, more relaxed, less pressured, more open to new experiences. You can expect the same from celibacy.

• During a vacation, you try new activities that you don't ordinarily try at home. During a period of celibacy, there are some things you can do that you can't when you're involved sexually:

—You can express all your *other* feelings.

—You can plunge into your work or your other interests without distraction or guilt.

—You can forget about birth control and still miss a period.

—You can dine with a friend and (1) eat as much as you want, (2) meet someone else afterward, (3) go home alone.

—You can become intimate friends with your intimates without negotiations.

—You can fall in love all over again, enjoy romance, court and be courted.

—While you are celibate, you can play with sexually active people.

• Don't tell everyone you are celibate. The resulting onslaught of sexual advances, no matter how subtle, will knock you out. The challenge is just too much for most sexually active people.

• Don't tell your parents that you are celibate if they are just getting used to your having sex. It's not fair.

• Celibacy by choice versus celibacy by default: It's best to decide that you want to take a vacation. Getting fired from work is not the same.

• Enjoy yourself. You'll probably have a lot of energy for a lot of things you've been thinking about doing.

• If sexual thoughts come up, don't attend to them. There's no sense being celibate if you make it a big strain for yourself. Thinking about sex constantly can be just as sexual as having sex. And not as rewarding.

• You can be celibate for as long a time as you want to be—for a week, a month, a year, or more. When you do return from vacation, everything will look fresh and new again.

When you stop being celibate, sex will have something new to offer you. Not only because you've been away, but because you are more settled within yourself. Or you can continue being on vacation if you're enjoying it. In either case, you can count on some very profound personal benefits to have occurred.

ACCEPTING CELIBACY

When we are taught "the rules" for sex, we need to learn not only what is socially acceptable and what might not be, but also that sex has an extended value that goes well beyond both its pleasure and procreative functions. The way to learn everything we ever wanted to know about sex is in the context of *full* knowledge of its range of expression— which must include celibacy. If we all have the potential to be celibate, then it is really a matter of finding out about and accepting this aspect of being sexual along with the active aspect of sex.

Whether it is a lifetime commitment under the guidance of a particular spiritual community or a two-week vacation in the bedroom of a married couple, celibacy is beginning to emerge in our society as a useful and positive vehicle to further personal growth for a number of people today. That this emergence is occurring in the midst of so many other social changes can lead to a great deal of speculation as to its causes. But there are two trends in particular that may be most important in understanding today's new celibacy. One is the obvious need to balance the uncomfortably heavy social focus on sexuality that continues to bombard this society—an overdoing for which two hundred years of sexual repression may no longer be a good excuse. The other is the steadily rising interest in religion and spiritual development. Celibacy may be one way for the individual and the society to resolve and integrate these two needs.

But if it is a social movement at all, it is a very private one. True, the new celibates are beginning to find and support each other. . . . They may even be old lovers reunited on a new basis. But there is no celibate "movement" as yet—no group of advocates on street corners with STOP signs. The men and women interviewed for this book were extremely private about their changed or changing sexuality. They may be pioneers, but they are not really ready to establish this new sexual frontier alone.

Gagnon and Simon found in their research on socialized sexuality that "Being the first to change [sexually] means dealing with certain kinds of anxieties and ambivalences." And Campbell observed that "No single person or couple can innovate a new style of sexual behavior, for sexuality is a complicated social phenomenon and always presupposes at least a minimally representative community as its basic unit." If this is the case, then we can assume that the practice of celibacy has a certain basic unit of at least latent social acceptance already or there would be no possibility for its advent in our society at this time.

What we are seeing now is a deepening of societal needs which can only be met by the deepening strength and increased creativity, intelligence, and happiness of each of us. As we grow in these values, all aspects of our development have to keep up and be integrated with each other. It is likely that this is why celibacy is surfacing—not for all of us—but for many who are ready for a more intimate, more flexible experience of love and a more balanced approach to living fulfilled, progressive lives.

Notes

Chapter 1

1. Milton Rugoff, *Prudery and Passion* (New York: Putnam, 1971), p. 378.
2. George Dullea, "A Lack of Sexual Desire Emerges as a Contemporary Condition," *The New York Times*, May 1, 1978, p. A18.
3. Carol Botwin, "Is There Sex after Marriage?," *The New York Times Magazine*, September 16, 1979, pp. 108–112.
4. Bertrand Russell, *Marriage and Morals* (New York: Bantam Books, 1968), pp. 9–10. First published in 1929.
5. Abraham Maslow, *Motivation and Personality* (New York: Harper & Row, 1970), pp. 187–188.
6. Elisabeth Haich, *Sexual Energy and Yoga* (New York: ASI Publishers, 1975), p. 52.
7. "How Our Passions and Hatreds Are Aroused," *San Francisco Chronicle,* September 18, 1978, p. 1.
8. Barbara Seaman, *Free and Female: The Sex Life of the Contemporary Woman* (New York: Coward, McCann, 1972), p. 191.
9. Michael Volin and Nancy Phelan, *Sex and Yoga* (New York: Harper & Row, 1967), p. 23.
10. H. J. Campbell, *The Pleasure Areas: A New Theory of Behavior* (New York: Delacorte Press, 1973), pp. 282, 292.

Chapter 2

1. Barbara W. Tuchman, *A Distant Mirror: The Calamitous Fourteenth Century* (New York: Alfred A. Knopf, 1978), p. 212.
2. Paul M. Conner, *Celibate Love* (Huntington, Ind.: Our Sunday Visitor, 1979), pp. 13–14.
3. Joe K. Adams, "The Love Taboo," in Herbert Otto, ed., *Love Today: A New Exploration* (New York: Association Press, 1972), p. 32.
4. A. C. Kinsey et al., *Sexual Behavior in the Human Female* (Philadelphia: Saunders, 1953), p. 625.
5. Charles Fracchia, *Living Together Alone: The New American Monasticism* (San Francisco: Harper & Row, 1979), pp. 124–125.

Chapter 3

1. William Masters and Virginia Johnson, *The Pleasure Bond* (Boston: Little, Brown, 1975), pp. 173–174.
2. Peter Koestenbaum, *Existential Sexuality: Choosing to Love* (Englewood Cliffs, N.J.: Prentice-Hall, 1974), pp. 17–18.
3. Abraham Maslow, "Love in Healthy People," in Ashley Montagu (ed.), *The Practice of Love* (Englewood Cliffs, N.J.: Prentice-Hall, 1975), pp. 108–109.
4. Herbert W. Richardson, *Nun, Witch, Playmate: The Americanization of Sex* (New York: Harper & Row, 1971), pp. 35–36.
5. Elisabeth Haich, *Sexual Energy and Yoga* (New York: ASI Publishers, 1975), p. 101.

Chapter 4

1. John Davenport, *Curiosities of Erotic Physiology* (New York: Robin Hood House, 1932).
2. A. C. Kinsey et al., *Sexual Behavior in the Human Female* (Philadelphia: Saunders, 1953), p. 612.
3. Hugo Beigel, "Romantic Love," in Ashley Montagu (ed.), *The Practice of Love* (Englewood Cliffs, N.J.: Prentice-Hall, 1975), p. 130.

4. Interview by Robert Levering, San Francisco *Bay Guardian*, November 23, 1978.

Chapter 5

1. Bertrand Russell, *Marriage and Morals* (New York: Bantam Books, 1968), p. 17.
2. Barbara Seaman, *Free and Female: The Sex Life of the Contemporary Woman* (New York: Coward, McCann, 1972), p. 210.
3. Helen Singer Kaplan, *The New Sex Therapy* (New York: Brunner/Mazel, 1974), p. 111.
4. Shere Hite, *The Hite Report* (New York: Macmillan, 1976), p. 205.
5. Ibid., p. 337.
6. June Singer, *Androgyny: Towards a New Theory of Sexuality* (Garden City, N.Y.: Doubleday Anchor, 1976), pp. 318–319.
7. Quoted in Paul Solomon, "The New Chastity," *Cosmopolitan*, January 1979.
8. Quoted in Enid Harlow, "Sexual Liberation Doesn't Always Mean Freedom," *Working Woman*, June 1977, p. 53.

Chapter 6

1. Ellen Frank and Carol Andersen, "How Important Is Sex to a Happy Marriage?," *Family Circle Magazine*, March 13, 1979.
2. Bertrand Russell, *Marriage and Morals* (New York: Bantam Books, 1968), p. 51.

Chapter 7

1. Julian Huxley, "The Direction of Human Development," in Ashley Montagu (ed.), *The Practice of Love* (Englewood Cliffs, N.J.: Prentice-Hall, 1975), p. 172.
2. June Singer, *Androgyny: Toward a New Theory of Sexuality* (Garden City, N.Y.: Doubleday Anchor, 1976), p. 270.
3. H. J. Campbell, *The Pleasure Areas: A New Theory of Behavior* (New York: Delacorte Press, 1973), p. 208.

4. Quoted in Irving Singer, *The Nature of Love: Plato to Luther* (New York: Random House, 1966), p. 271.
5. Mary S. Calderone, "Sexuality—A Creative Force," in Herbert Otto (ed.), *The New Sexuality* (Palo Alto, Calif.: Science and Behavior Books, 1971), pp. 269–270.

Chapter 8

1. Bertrand Russell, *Marriage and Morals* (New York: Bantam Books, 1968), p. 27.
2. Elisabeth Haich, *Sexual Energy and Yoga* (New York: ASI Publishers, 1975), pp. 130–131.
3. Mircea Eliade, *Yoga, Immortality and Freedom* (New York: Pantheon, 1958), p. 254.
4. Aldous Huxley, *Island* (New York: Harper, 1962), p. 137.

Bibliography

Arieti, Silvano and James A. Arieti. *Love Can Be Found.*
New York: Harcourt Brace Jovanovich, 1977.

Bailey, D. S. *Sexual Relations in Christian Thought.* New
York: Harper, 1959.

Bianchi, Eugene. "America as Monastery," *Commonweal*
(March 1, 1974), 530–531.

Beigel, Hugo. "Romantic Love," in Ashley Montagu (ed.),
The Practice of Love. Englewood Cliffs, N.J.: Prentice-
Hall, 1975.

Blofeld, John. *The Secret and the Sublime: Taoist Mysteries
and Magic.* New York: E. P. Dutton, 1973.

Burrows, Millar. *Burrows on the Dead Sea Scrolls.* Grand
Rapids, Mich.: Baker Books, 1978.

Campbell, H. J. *The Pleasure Areas: A New Theory of Behavior.* New York: Delacorte Press, 1973.

Chaucard, Paul. *Our Need of Love.* New York: P. J.
Kenedy, 1968.

Colton, Helen. *Sex after the Sexual Revolution.* New York:
Association Press, 1972.

Eliade, Mircea. *Yoga, Immortality and Freedom.* New York:
Pantheon Books, 1958.

Fracchia, Charles. *Living Together Alone: The New American Monasticism.* Harper & Row, San Francisco, 1979.

Fellman, Sheldon and Paul Neimark. *The Virile Man.* New
York: Stein & Day, 1976.

Freud, Sigmund. *Civilization and Its Discontents*. New York: W. W. Norton, 1962.

Fromm, Erich. *The Art of Loving*. New York: Harper & Row, 1962.

Gagnon, John H. and William Simon. *Sexual Conduct: The Social Sources of Human Sexuality*. Chicago: Aldine, 1973.

Goergen, Donald. *The Sexual Celibate*. New York: Seabury, 1974.

Gould, Arthur and F. L. DuBois. *The Science of Sex Regeneration*. Chicago: Advanced Thought Co., 1911.

Haich, Elisabeth. *Sexual Energy and Yoga*. New York: ASI Publishers, 1975.

Hite, Shere. *The Hite Report*. New York: Macmillan, 1976.

Hunt, Morton. *Sexual Behavior in the 1970s*. Chicago: Playboy Press, 1974.

Huxley, Aldous. *Island*. New York: Harper, 1962.

Kinsey, A. C., W. B. Pomeroy, and C. E. Martin. *Sexual Behavior in the Human Female*. Philadelphia: Saunders, 1953.

——, ——, ——. *Sexual Behavior in the Human Male*. Philadelphia: Saunders, 1948.

Koestenbaum, Peter. *Existential Sexuality: Choosing to Love*. Englewood Cliffs, N.J.: Prentice-Hall, 1974.

Laski, Marghanita. *Ecstasy: A Study of Some Secular and Religious Experiences*. Westport, Conn.: Greenwood Press, 1968.

Lea, Henry C. *History of Sacerdotal Celibacy in the Christian Church*. London: Watts, 1932.

Lederer, William J. and Don D. Jackson. *The Mirages of Marriage*. New York: W. W. Norton, 1968.

Lewis, C. S. *The Four Loves*. London: Collins, 1960.

Maslow, A. "Love in Healthy People," in Ashley Montagu (ed.), *The Practice of Love*, Englewood Cliffs, N.J.: Prentice-Hall, 1975.

——. *Motivation and Personality*. New York: Harper & Row, 1970.

Masters, William and Virginia Johnson. *Human Sexual Response*. Boston: Little, Brown, 1966.

——, and ——. *The Pleasure Bond: A New Look at Sexuality and Commitment*. Boston: Little, Brown, 1975.

May, Rollo. *Love and Will.* New York: W. W. Norton, 1969.

Menninger, Walter. *Happiness Without Sex and Other Things Too Good to Miss.* New York: Sheed, Andrews and McMeel, 1976.

Meyer, J. J. *Sexual Life in Ancient India.* New York: Barnes & Noble, 1953.

Money, John and Patricia Tucker. *Sexual Signatures.* Boston: Little, Brown, 1975.

Montagu, Ashley (ed.). *The Practice of Love.* Englewood Cliffs, N.J.: Prentice-Hall, 1975.

————. *Touching: The Human Significance of Skin.* New York: Harper & Row, 1972.

Otto, Herbert A. *Love Today: A New Exploration.* New York: Association Press, 1972.

————. *The New Sexuality.* Palo Alto, Calif.: Science and Behavior Books, 1971.

Richardson, Herbert W. *Nun, Witch, Playmate: The Americanization of Sex.* New York: Harper & Row, 1971.

Roberta, Sister M. "A Sister Considers Chastity," *America* (April 10, 1965).

Rosenbaum, Jean B., "A Psychoanalyst's Case for Celibacy," *Catholic World* (May 1967).

Rosner, Fred. *Sex Ethics in the Writings of Moses Maimonides.* New York: Bloch Publishing Co., 1974.

Rugoff, Milton. *Prudery and Passion: Sexuality in Victorian America.* New York: Putnam, 1971.

Russell, Bertrand. *Marriage and Morals.* New York: Liveright, 1929; Bantam Books, 1968.

Sadler, William A. *Existence and Love: A New Approach in Existential Phenomenology.* New York: Scribner, 1970.

Seaman, Barbara. *Free and Female: The Sex Life of the Contemporary Woman.* New York: Coward, McCann, 1972.

Slater, Philip. *Footholds: Understanding the Shifting Sexual and Family Tensions in Our Culture.* New York: Dutton, 1977.

Singer, Irving. *The Nature of Love: Plato to Luther.* New York: Random House, 1966.

Singer, June. *Androgyny: Toward a New Theory of Sexuality.* Garden City, N.Y.: Anchor Press/Doubleday, 1976.

Sullivan, Harry S. *Interpersonal Theory of Psychiatry.* New York: W. W. Norton, 1953.

Teilhard de Chardin, Pierre. *Human Energy.* New York: Harcourt Brace Jovanovich, 1970.

Volin, Michael and Nancy Phelan. *Sex and Yoga.* New York: Harper & Row, 1967.

Wade, Joseph D. *Chastity, Sexuality and Personal Hang-Ups.* New York: Alba House, 1971.

Zilbergeld, Bernard. *Male Sexuality: A Guide to Personal Fulfillment.* Boston: Little, Brown, 1977.